all
about ARCHAEOLOGY

Wooden carving of a stag, preserved in ice in a Scythian tomb of the fourth century B.C. at Pazyryk, Western Siberia.

all
about
ARCHAEOLOGY

Lloyd and Jennifer Laing

W. H. Allen · London and New York · 1977
(A Howard & Wyndham Company)

Copyright © 1977 by Lloyd and Jennifer Laing

Filmset in Monophoto Times 11 on 13 pt. by
Richard Clay (The Chaucer Press), Ltd., Bungay, Suffolk
and printed in Great Britain by
Fletcher & Son Ltd., Norwich
for the publishers
W. H. Allen & Co. Ltd.,
44 Hill Street, London W1X 8LB

ISBN 0 491 02440 1

CONTENTS

ACKNOWLEDGEMENTS

THE AUTHORS AND PUBLISHERS would like to thank the following individuals and institutions for permission to use illustrations that have appeared in this book: the School of Archaeology and Oriental Studies, Liverpool University; the Department of the Environment (Crown Copyright Reserved); Miss Felicity Kinross and the British Broadcasting Corporation; Dr John Coles and the Somerset Levels Project, the Department of Archaeology and Anthropology, Cambridge University; Professor Stuart Piggott; Miss Nancy Edwards; Miss Pamela Perrie; the Silkeborg Museum; the Statens Sjöhistorika Museum, Wasavarret, Stockholm; the Hermitage Museum, Leningrad; and the Trustees of the British Museum.

PREFACE

ALMOST EVERYTHING PEOPLE did in the past can leave some trace, either as objects, or such flimsy evidence as changes in soil colour. People have left us their treasures to marvel at, their houses and tombs, their works of art. Somewhere in the world almost every type of apparently perishable material has survived—papyrus from Egypt, loaves of bread from the lava-covered city of Pompeii, human bodies from the ice of the Steppes, or the embalmed remains of the Egyptian god-kings. Some men committed crimes which they hoped would be undetected, but which, after thousands of years, were discovered by scientific investigations. Detectives of the past use a variety of complex techniques and many subjects to piece together the clues our ancestors left behind. Sometimes the study is so involved that it may seem as if they are relying on guesswork. Some of the processes are outlined in this book, along with some of the results of the research.

The past is all around us, though often ignored or unnoticed. Without a knowledge of the past, however, the present cannot be put into its true perspective. Hatreds and mistrusts, alliances or customs are often deeply rooted in antiquity and it is helpful to understand their origins. Resentments between countries, for instance, can be harboured for centuries and often have no place in modern society. In contrast, some new ideas will be found to be very ancient indeed. Take, for instance, Britain's entry into the Common Market, which seemed such a huge step at the time to many Britons. Only 2,000 years ago (very recently in the development of Man), not only was Britain friendly with the Continent, but the first king whose name we know —Divitiacus—actually held lands on each side of the Channel. Britain's 'isolation' from the Continent was something that had grown up only fairly recently in history.

It can be highly instructive therefore, to look to the past to find out how people solved various problems—it is not human beings who have changed so much as the technology they are capable of maintaining. The basic needs of society remain remarkably similar throughout history.

1 GATHERING THE CLUES

ABOUT 1,200 YEARS AGO A MAN was walking through the stone ruins of an ancient city. The high walls, towering above his head, were weathered and covered with ivy and lichen. Every now and then the remnants of what had once been fine wall paintings peeped out of the foliage. The man probably stumbled a few times on the uneven ground and his clumsy feet dislodged some of the stones. They were coloured and flattened and made a pattern when he scraped away the dirt that had accumulated during the centuries. There were figures of animals, sea creatures and other signs and symbols that he did not understand. As he continued his walk, he had to be careful not to fall into the open stone-lined pools which had once flowed with warm water from the natural hot springs. He was a simple man, probably a priest. He had been taught to read and write, but there his education had stopped. He had never learned about the history of the area and had no means of finding out who had built the ruins, or when. Overcome by the sadness of the buildings, he returned home, and taking up a feather pen, dipped in wood-dye ink, he began to write on a piece of vellum:

This is a wondrous wall; smashed by chance, defences

Artist's reconstruction of the temple of Minerva, at Bath, Somerset, as it might have appeared in the eighth century A.D.

have perished: the work of giants is decaying. Roofs have fallen, the towers and their gates are ruined: there is rime on their mortar, the roofs are broken, shattered, undermined through age. The mighty builders have perished and lie within the earth, the strong grasp of the earth: since then a hundred generations have passed away.

The writer was wrong of course. The ruins were not built by giants, nor were they as old as 100 generations (about 2,500 years). The *Ruin*, one of the finest of all Old English poems, is usually taken to refer to the ancient Roman ruins at Bath, Somerset, as they appeared in the eighth century A.D.

The Romans had left some 300 years before the writer of the *Ruin* was alive—their legions had been withdrawn from Britain to the Continent in about A.D. 409. New settlers, the Saxons, had arrived in Somerset in about A.D. 577 and almost a hundred years later their king, Osric, founded a Christian community for both men and women.

The site chosen for the monastic settlement was the ruined city of **Aquae Sulis** (modern Bath). The writer of the poem was almost certainly one of these Christians. The walls and fragments of mosaic floors were probably all that remained of the Roman city.

But how do we know that the writer was wrong? If people living only three hundred years after the Romans had left had no idea who had built Bath, how does twentieth-century man know so much?

The answer lies in the study of things that have survived from the past—archaeology.

Methods of Studying the Past

There are many methods of studying the past, and the archaeologist makes use of them all. **Geology** is the study of the earth's formation—when rocks and mountains came into existence—and deals with remote periods in time, up to 2,800 million years ago. **History** is the study of written records. From analysing the things that men wrote down it is often possible to find out how they thought, what they did and when. At first this might seem an infallible way of studying man's past. But historical evidence can have drawbacks. Writing was not invented until about 5,000 years ago—comparatively recently in the 3–4 million years that man has probably walked the earth. Even after this date, only men in civilised societies needed to write. The less complicated the society, the less the need for written communication. The period before writing was used, in any society, is called **prehistory**, and varies from place to place. In North America, prehistory ends with Columbus's voyage of discovery in 1492 and in the settlements of Europeans that followed, but in Britain it ends with the Roman invasion of A.D. 43. Prehistory is studied almost entirely

from archaeology, though very remote periods are helped
by geological research as well.

Even when written records exist it is not always easy to
study the past. Several scripts have not yet been deciphered.
Sometimes people did not write down things that were
true—either unintentionally or deliberately. The Romans,
for instance, rarely admitted to failure if one of their forts
was sacked. The building inscription would be more likely
to read 'This fort was rebuilt after it had decayed through
age'. It is possible that the writer of the *Ruin* knew that
the Romans and not giants had built the walls at Bath, but
if he did, he did not say so.

People who had a highly organised way of life usually left
written records—lists of kings or taxes, prayers or laws for
instance. It is rare, however, for written records like these
to explain the ordinary details of everyday life. Archaeology
is invaluable for filling in the gaps and in some cases
verifying written accounts.

Human beings leave an amazing assortment of material
behind them. People lose things in their gardens, in their
fields, their public buildings and their houses. They throw
their rubbish into waste tips or dung and ash heaps, and
sometimes even use disused houses for the purpose. Some
people did not bother too much where they put their rubbish
and were happy for it to be trodden into the hard-packed
earth floors. In times of stress, before banks were used,
people put their valuables under the ground. Sometimes
they were unable to return to retrieve them. Some people
threw objects into bogs or springs to appease local gods,
others defaced buildings or destroyed works of art. Mankind has changed the environment by digging ditches and
cutting down trees, by building dams and diverting rivers.
Stone has been quarried and clay removed. Wood and clay,

Panel from an Egyptian wooden coffin from Beni Hassan, with inscription of magical formulae for the dead, *c.* 2000 B.C.

stone and bone have been fashioned into objects men can use. Human beings are remarkably versatile, and have engaged in an astonishing number of activites. By studying the things people invented or modified, threw away or hid, the buildings they erected or razed to the ground, the archaeologist can build up a detailed picture of life in the past—often clearer than the picture most people have of the world they live in today. A study of the past and the way human beings have developed can lead to greater understanding of the modern world; for example, the way laws and customs, boundaries of states and societies were formed. Sometimes it is even possible to predict what might happen in the future and if necessary to take preventive measures by studying similar situations from the past.

In order to study old places and objects, the archaeologist uses experts on almost any subject. If an archaeologist found, for instance, that some fine jet bracelets had been manufactured on a site he was excavating, he would immediately call on the assistance of a geologist. From a study of the possible sources of the jet, it might be possible to discover which trade routes were being used. A palaeobotanist would be able to analyse any seeds or pollens found and could build up a picture of the countryside—what is today open grassland might have been dense forest two thousand years ago. Zoologists and biologists study bones and plant remains; metallurgists can work out where ores were mined and how they were forged. Computers are often used to analyse objects that appear almost identical to the human eye—such as the thousands of flint tools used by Stone Age man. The list is almost endless—lawyers, historians, food technologists, sociologists, doctors and many others have all produced valuable archaeological work. In the last few centuries millions of fragments of objects have been analysed, compared and discussed. Experiments and excavations have been carried out and researchers have toiled in libraries, museums and on excavations. Archaeology has become such a vast subject that it has become divided into specialist studies according to period (e.g. Prehistoric, Dark Ages, Medieval), or area (e.g. South American, Egyptian, Greek), or type (e.g. industrial, underwater).

In order to make the apparently simple statement that the writer of the *Ruin* was wrong about the builders of Aquae Sulis, several centuries of work by scholars and amateurs have been amassed.

2 HOW THINGS BECOME LOST AND BURIED

IN 1954 A YOUNG MAN WAS wandering through the very same city that had so impressed the writer of the *Ruin*. He was very hot and bored, but although there were many walls and baths to be seen they were not those seen by the poet. Aquae Sulis, the Roman spa city (built on natural springs), had been obliterated and replaced by a splendid eighteenth and nineteenth century town. All that could be seen of the original city was a few walls and drains that had been uncovered by the builders of the modern city and which ran tantalisingly under the concrete. The young man, Barry Cunliffe, immediately became interested in the mystery. Nearly ten years later he returned. By then he was lecturer in archaeology at Bristol University (he is now professor at Oxford), and with him was a team of archaeologists. Together they excavated up to twelve feet below the modern street level and uncovered the remains of the buildings that had been seen by the writer of the *Ruin*. Under the baths and the elegant rooms where Georgian and Regency ladies had sampled the waters and made polite conversation they found the ruins of a temple, the finest to be discovered in Britain so far. In the cavern-like depths near the hot springs his team worked in sweltering heat under lights and with the continuous hum of the pumps

The Great Bath at Bath, Somerset, as it is today.

which removed water from the excavation area. But they
were rewarded for their hard work. In the spring was an
amazing assortment of objects—left there as offerings to
the Roman goddess sixteen centuries before.

After just a few months of excavation the archaeologists
had found out more about the city of Aquae Sulis than even
the Romans would have known. As they sweated in the hot
baths or chatted with their friends the Roman people would
have given little thought to how their workmen had constructed the temple, or how many offerings had been made
to the goddess.

From inscriptions that have been found, even the names
of some of the Roman inhabitants of Bath are known.
Lucius Vitellius Tancinus was a citizen of Caurium in
Spain. He died aged 46, after 26 years in the army and was
buried at Aquae Sulis. A small child died there too, at the
age of 3 years, 4 months and 9 days. Her name was
Successa Petronia and her mother was Victoria Sabina.

Sand encroaching on a Roman mosaic at Knossos, Crete, despite the shelter of a modern shed.

The Romans obviously led a highly organised way of life. They were able to communicate across a vast empire stretching from the River Euphrates in the east to Scotland in the north. Yet within a few hundred years only vague memories of their four centuries of rule in Britain remained in the minds of the inhabitants.

How were the remains of Roman Bath buried in the twelve hundred years or so between the writing of the *Ruin* and the modern excavations? How is it possible for baths and buildings that were famous from Egypt to Germany to disappear so completely that archaeologists have to dig to uncover the remains?

The answer is very simple. The remains are covered either by the work of the weather or by man, or by a combination of both.

Weathering and the Formation of the Soil

The earth's surface is never static. All the time material is eroded from some areas and deposited in others. Natural deposits can be hundreds of feet thick and any buildings

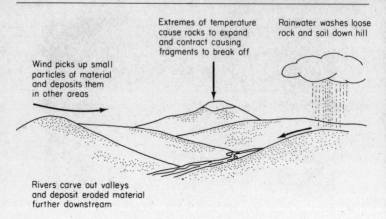

The effect of weathering on the landscape.

can be buried completely unless deliberately kept cleared. This can be seen happening in a dramatic way in sandy areas where sand dunes often encroach on modern settlements (see page 17).

Eventually, the fragments of rock, clay or sand mix with the remains of dead plants and animals and form soil. Soil is usually only a few feet deep and can be non-existent in exposed mountainous regions where material is removed and not deposited.

Wind and water can wear away stone buildings and can cause timber structures to rot away completely. Once the buildings have collapsed, natural deposits may cover them, and eventually a layer of soil may form and vegetation will take a hold. The depth of deposits over an area depends on the local conditions and the length of time during which deposition has taken place.

Eventually the walls or ditches will be completely hidden under the new landscape.

Earthworms

Earthworms play an important part in burying ancient
remains. These insignificant looking creatures help to aerate
and fertilise the soil. They live in underground burrows
which they produce by eating soil. The earthworms digest
minerals from the soil which is then disgorged into empty
burrows, spaces in the soil, or in some cases at the surface.

Two types of earthworm (out of the 25 species in Britain)
take discarded soil to the ground surface and deposit it in
'casts'. They are *Allolobophora longa* and *Allolobophora
nocturna*. This small proportion amounts to an enormous
number of earthworms. It has been estimated that there can
be a total number of between half and 3 million earthworms to the acre (about 100 per square yard). The weight
of the earthworms below ground can equal that of the
livestock above.

In ten years earthworms can move up to $2\frac{1}{2}$ inches of
soil to the surface. Any pieces of jewellery or pottery,
for instance, lost in 1960, could be up to 4 inches below
the surface today simply because of worm action.

Earthworm action does have its limits, however. Earthworms do not like to burrow in rubbly or acid soils, nor
are they happy below about eight inches from the surface
(although they can go to a depth of about six feet). If
natural or man-made deposition of material occurs, the
earthworms simply migrate upwards. The disturbance of
material by worm action is thus lessened once objects are
buried to about 8 inches below ground level. However,
although an object, or the floor of an ancient building, may
be several feet underground, it will not necessarily have been
undisturbed by earthworms in the past.

Earthworms can bring small objects to the surface where
the rain washes them, so they are visible and easily found

After sixteen centuries, even Roman fort walls 20 ft. high succumb
to the elements at Richborough, Kent

by observers with keen eyes. The Appendix explains what
should be done with any man-made objects (broken fragments of pottery, glass, ironwork, wood, or bone for
instance) that are found.

Human Activity

The work of man is as important in burying sites as the
forces of nature, although the weather always has some part
to play.

When a building is abandoned, the weather gets to work.
Usually, the roof is the first to collapse, followed by the
walls. The wind and rain will deposit organic and mineral
material, soil will form and plants will start to grow. In
some cases, however, if the building was particularly well
sited, perhaps being near water or an important trade route,
the site itself might not be completely abandoned. This
happens frequently today—areas of cities are cleared of old
houses for rebuilding to take place. The old buildings are

deliberately demolished, and the rubble is used for the new
foundations. If a long period elapses between the demolition
and the rebuilding, a natural layer of soil may form. This
is what happened at Bath. The town does not seem to have
been abandoned completely after the Romans left, and had
been subjected to several phases of building. For this reason,
Barry Cunliffe and his excavators had to dig to uncover the
past.

Stratigraphy

The layers of material which build up on an ancient site,
whether by man-made or natural causes, are the archaeologist's clues to the past. Every time a new floor or yard,
house foundation or hearth, road or public square is laid
down, the earth is thrown up and deposited elsewhere in
the same way as natural deposits. The different layers of
material thus formed can be many feet thick (the ramparts
at Maiden Castle, an Iron Age hillfort in Dorset, for
example, are over 100 feet high), or almost non-existent
(such as the thin layers that build up on an earth floor).

A study of layers is called **stratigraphy**. Each layer is distinguished from the others by differences in texture and
colour. It is part of the excavation art to be able to
recognise the layers and to interpret them. On some sites
the differences between each layer are very slight and can
be missed completely if not professionally excavated. The
most recent layers to be laid down are at the top. An
excavation uncovers the story of what happened on the site
in reverse order.

Post-holes and Pits

Layers of soil are rarely put down neatly—sometimes
material simply fills in holes. Man digs holes in the ground

Two squared and one rounded post-hole during excavations at
Lochmaben Castle, Scotland, in 1971. In the background the
edge of a ditch is visible.

for many reasons—for containing rubbish, for drains,
gullies, house foundations, posts, stakes, fences, etc.

Although it is easy to fill in and cover a pit or post-hole
with earth so the surface looks much the same as its surroundings, it is practically impossible (even with the aid of
a computer) to replace the earth exactly in the same
position. In practice no one would make the attempt. The
soil that fills the dug-out area is usually less closely packed
than that around. Often it will be a different colour if the
hole was filled in some time after it was dug. Therefore, if
an archaeologist finds patches of ground that are roughly
rectangular or round and are of a different colour or texture
from the surrounding areas, he will suspect that they were
once holes in the ground and will treat them accordingly.

Sometimes, the posts or stakes that were in the holes were
removed in antiquity (perhaps to be used elsewhere), in

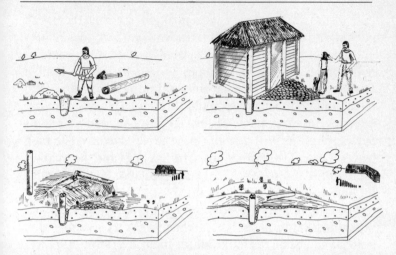

which case the filling usually differs markedly from the surrounding soil. At other times the posts may have rotted in position. Minerals will be washed down into the rotted remains of the post and eventually a very rich soil will form in the place of the post. This will be different in colour and texture to the filling which kept the post in position in its hole.

Rabbits and voles can often complicate stratigraphy. Many a promising post-hole has been excavated carefully, only for it to turn an impossible U-bend at the bottom and carry on in a series of loops and circles dug out by animals. Sometimes animals try to 'improve' on features they find underground—they will start tunnelling in a true post-hole where the soil is softer and easier to dig, and then continue into undisturbed soil. After a few years, the tunnel may become infilled and almost indistinguishable from the post-hole itself in colour and texture.

The illustrations above show what might happen to the ground in the very common operation of building a wooden house. The man digs the holes to take the posts,

then places the wooden posts in position, securing them with
packing stones. He then builds the walls with wooden planks
and adds a thatched roof. Eventually, after some years of
living in the house, it becomes too small for his family.
During this time a layer of dirt and domestic rubbish will
have built up in and around the structure. (Domestic refuse
includes little fragments of broken pottery, beads, a child's
toy perhaps, as well as more perishable objects.) The man
leaves the hut for another house he has built and the weather
eventually causes the original hut to collapse. The soil builds
up and vegetation takes a hold.

This is a very simple situation of course. There are many
other possibilities, and the archaeologist excavating such
a site would be on the look-out for them. The stratigraphical
evidence on some sites is extraordinarily complex. Some
medieval abbeys, for instance, have dozens of floors within
a depth of a few inches. Each one will have a distinctive
texture or colour. Sites which have been occupied for many
centuries can have the remains of hundreds of huts or
houses. The post-holes or pits from some huts can cut down
through the layers left by much earlier structures. Sometimes, existing buildings in disrepair were refurbished and
lived in. The interpretation of the meaning of the layers
is a complex process, which takes a lot of experience to
learn.

Dramatic Losses and Discoveries

Sometimes, natural forces can produce dramatic obliter-
ation of buildings. In A.D. 79, the volcano Vesuvius erupted.
Many of the small Italian settlements on its slopes were
covered. Amongst them was the fine city of Pompeii, which
was covered with tens of feet of molten lava. People were
encased as they ran, a dog curled up in agony and a young

girl crept into the shelter of an older woman's arms, hoping to escape the holocaust. Although life in the city was destroyed, paradoxically the structures were preserved by the very lava which struck down the inhabitants (see p. 118).

Natural forces can also cover sites and reveal them later. Such was the case of Skara Brae, in Orkney. Here, in the winter of 1850, a fierce storm tore the grass from sand dunes and whirled up the sand to lay bare the walls of a prehistoric village. The site was partially investigated, but it was not until another storm in 1925 revealed still more of the lost village that archaeologists began to explore the remains scientifically. The excavations carried out then and more recently, proved that the village had been occupied over 4,000 years ago. Due to the shortage of wood on the island, the villagers had built everything of stone, including the furniture. It is still possible to wander through the empty houses with their stone beds, dressers and hearths. The drains and the strange carvings on the walls of the passages that led between the houses are still visible. The passages were covered, and the entire village was found to have been covered by refuse which, presumably, insulated it from the bitter northern winds. The inhabitants were very conscious of hygiene, however—the drainage system was very elaborate.

The village of Skara Brae met its end, like Pompeii 2,000 years later, in catastrophe. A storm had blown choking sand along the passages and into the houses. One woman in her haste caught her necklace on the door as she raced along the passage. The beads fell in a trail behind her and remained in position for nearly four millennia. Many people abandoned their prized possessions where they were hidden under the mattresses in the stone-lined beds. A few people returned to the ghost village after the disaster, but Skara

The interior of a house at Skara Brae, Orkney, showing furniture,
occupied around 2000 B.C.

Brae was dead, and gradually the sand covered it up entirely
and it was forgotten.

Removal of material is not always so uniform. In 1938,
a mound containing the burial of an Anglo-Saxon ship was
excavated at Sutton Hoo in Suffolk. It lay near the River
Deben, adjacent to several other mounds, most of which
had been disturbed in the seventeenth century when grave
robbers had dug through and removed the treasures. A hole
had been hacked into the ship's burial mound where the
treasure was estimated to lie. The robbers found nothing.
Yet the mound contained one of the finest and most important treasures that has ever been discovered in Europe.
The grave robbers had missed the true centre of the mound
because one end had been eroded badly through human
and possibly rabbit activity. The mound was smaller than
it had been originally, and what had appeared to be the
middle was, in fact, near one end.

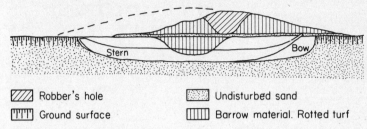

Diagram of the Sutton Hoo ship under the denuded mound showing robber's trench to one side of the true burial chamber in the centre of the ship.

Sometimes, entire civilisations can be forgotten and covered by natural means. Many are remembered in legends or folk-lore, but others disappear completely. This normally happens when disaster falls—the inhabitants flee or are killed and the area may be abandoned for centuries before others, with no knowledge of the history of the place, move in. Sometimes, the overthrow of the central power in a civilisation may lead to the old way of life being forgotten as the people adjust to the new conquerors. While the manuscript of this book was being typed, a new civilisation, in the Middle East, Ebla, has been claimed to have been discovered. Although it had been powerful over a large area, it had been almost totally obliterated from memory (see p. 141).

3 WHAT MATERIALS SURVIVE

burial at Sutton Hoo, Suffolk, was truly princely. The remains of a mailcoat, a fine decorated helmet, a splendid gold buckle weighing nearly 15 ounces, a gold and garnet purse containing gold coins, gold and garnet clasps to secure clothing at the shoulders, a silver dish and silver bowls, a rusted iron sword with a rich gold and garnet pommel, and bronze and enamel bowls for hanging from chains, were among the finds. All these were objects that optimistic archaeologists might hope to discover in the burial chamber of a pagan Saxon prince. But one thing puzzled scholars for years. There was no body in the mound.

This mystery led to many theories being put forward. Had the prince been lost at sea? Was the mound therefore a cenotaph, not a grave? Had the prince been a Christian? It was not customary to bury Christians with worldly possessions. If the prince had been buried in a simple Christian grave somewhere else, perhaps his pagan followers had built the traditional mound, so he should not suffer what in their eyes would have been dishonour. More likely still, a theory which has been in favour for several years is that the body was once in the mound, but had perished without a trace. During the time that this book has been written a further hypothesis has been forwarded. Scientific analysis of some charred bone that was found in the large silver dish suggests that the prince had been cremated. The bones had been so badly damaged, however, that their identity was not recognised for over 30 years.

This story illustrates clearly the sort of problems that can occur and the kind of wrong answers that can be given, because of the simple fact that some substances survive better than others.

The survival of objects depends on a very complex series of chemical, physical and biological reactions in their surroundings. Metal or bone objects are obviously more durable than objects such as bodies, paper, wood, or leather under normal conditions in temperate climates. Extremes of climate or local conditions can cause some apparently durable substances to disintegrate entirely, and other, apparently perishable materials, to be preserved.

The Effect of the Soil
The make-up of the soil is of prime importance to the survival of any lost object. Once formed, soil can vary according to the original parent rock and with the climate. It can be acid or alkaline (**basic**), or salty to various degrees. Soil can range from very light and porous to heavy and impervious, or from well-drained to waterlogged. The climate can subject soil to constant deluges of water which wash minerals downwards or weather away more of the parent rock; to constant heat and rain (as in equatorial forests); or to alternating high and low temperatures. Organic material such as paper or wood disintegrates very rapidly in equatorial conditions, but can remain almost intact in the dry airtight conditions of Egyptian tombs.

This Roman scent bottle made of green glass has survived from the early second century A.D.

Except within broad limits, the effect that burial will have on objects is unpredictable.

Acid soils can cause glass to peel off in layers like an onion skin. Limestones or plasters can be eroded chemically. The preservation of bone in acid conditions depends partly on the age, sex and health of the individual. Bone is made up of calcium phosphate, some calcium carbonate and other salts, and organic material. Under acid conditions (especially in porous soils), the phosphate can be entirely leached (washed) out, leaving little or no trace of the bone. Bones can be reduced to a shadow if some of the components are removed chemically. They are thus very difficult to detect even under very careful excavation conditions. A 'shadow' skeleton was skilfully revealed by Professor Stuart Piggott at Corrimony in Inverness, during the excavation of a prehistoric chambered tomb, dating from around 1800 B.C.

The effect of acid soils on metals can be so drastic that iron can completely dissolve. Copper and its alloys can be reduced to the green-blue copper acetate, **verdigris**, often visible only as a faint stain in the soil.

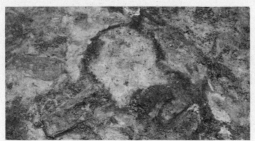

Close-up of the head of the Corrimony skeleton. The skull shows
up as a light, roughly circular area in the centre.

A badly corroded piece of iron. Its identity was a mystery until
metallurgical tests were carried out proving that it was originally
a blade. From excavations at the Mote of Mark, 1973 (page 145).

Two coins in different states of preservation. *Left,* silver tetra-
drachm of Athens, fifth century B.C. *Right,* Roman bronze coin
of early fourth century A.D.

Bronze neck of a Roman flagon. Most bronze vessels disintegrate due to the thin walls. The thick neck is often all that survives.

Roman pottery lamp from Syria with a white powdery deposit of lime acquired prior to discovery.

Alkaline soils cause glass to disintegrate more quickly than in acid conditions because of its chemical make-up. Even flint, usually very durable, can acquire a white crust (**patina**) and metals can be broken down chemically.

Salty soils can cause painted wall plaster to disintegrate: the paint flakes off the plaster. Ivory survives under many conditions but can be flaked off in onion skin layers as a result of salt in the soil. The rusting of iron is speeded up by the presence of salt. However, once silver has acquired its dark brown tarnishing it will be protected by this coating and will deteriorate no further.

Unburied Sites

In arid climates, the wind can beat against the stones with small fragments of sand, abrading like sandpaper, wearing the stone away slowly over the centuries. In moist warm (tropical or equatorial) climates, rainwater will erode the stones, and expansion and contraction in the warm of the day and the cool of the night, will also weather them away.

Industrially polluted air can cause pieces of stone to fall off buildings. The Elgin Marbles were carved in the fifth century B.C. and were placed in a frieze around the top of the temple of Athene (better known as the Parthenon) in Athens. Some were taken to the British Museum by Lord Elgin between 1802 and 1812. Casts were taken of those which were left behind. Those which were left exposed in the Parthenon have deteriorated more in the last 150 years than in the previous 2,000 and the details cannot be recognised except from the casts. The Marbles in the British Museum are still in good condition.

Airtight Conditions

The Old Stone Age paintings in the cave at Lascaux, in France, survived almost perfectly through 20,000 years of airtight conditions underground. Since their discovery in 1941, the breath of visitors has led to the growth of fungus on the paintings, causing them to deteriorate. The cave has now been closed and sealed off except for rare instances when visitors are allowed inside.

In many rock-cut or man-made tombs a minimum of oxygen is admitted. The growth of organisms as well as the decay of organic material (such as bodies, paper, wood) is

inhibited. The tomb of Tutankhamun, possibly the most
famous Egyptian burial, shows this clearly. When the tomb
was opened in 1922, some damp was found to have pene-
trated the thick limestone walls. Fungus had affected all
the colours in the wall paintings except yellow. Tests showed
that the artist had achieved the yellow colour by the use
of orpiment (arsenic sulphide) which was toxic to the fungus.

Once such airtight containers are opened and the air is
allowed to circulate freely, the contents rapidly deteriorate
unless treated. Thousands of mummies and other Egyptian
finds were lost in this way in the antiquaries' looting
expeditions in the seventeenth, eighteenth and nineteenth
centuries.

Very Dry Conditions

In 1900 at Niya in Khotan, a desert region between India
and China, Sir Aurel Stein found a settlement that had been
occupied just before A.D. 300. Around the wooden houses
he found the remains of gardens, with the dried-out avenues
and arbours of poplar trees and orchards of plum, apricot
and mulberry. The timber framework of the houses and the
plastered matting that was used to make the walls were
preserved in the dry climate.

As he cleared the rooms of sand, Stein found the things
that had been left by the departing occupants—one small
cupboard contained a bow, a bundle of wooden spears, part
of a wooden shield, wooden spindles and a wooden walking
stick which was so well preserved he used it. In another
room were wooden tablets for writing on (some inscribed),
tamarisk pens, wooden chopsticks and a rush hammock.
A broken guitar still had some string intact; a carved
wooden chair, a mousetrap, some broken brooms and a
shoe-last were testimony to the lives led by the occupants.

Part of the clothing of a sixth-century ecclesiastic from Coptic Egypt, well-preserved from the dry conditions.

Felt, textiles and patterned rugs were tattered but their original colours were still preserved. Outside the houses the rubbish heaps still had a strong smell, but the excavator gallantly persevered and was rewarded with the finding of a series of documents on sheepskin. All these objects had been dried out and thus preserved by the climatic conditions.

Only slightly less dramatic are the remains of the 'Basket Maker' Indians who lived between the fourth and ninth centuries A.D. in caves and overhanging rocks in Arizona. Because of the dry conditions, the bodies of their dead have been found mummified, from which it is possible to study even such details as basket-maker hairstyles. The baskets which give the people their name are common finds. So too are feathered ornaments, textiles, rabbit snares, leather bags and pouches, feathered darts and planting sticks.

Dry conditions in Egypt have led to the preservation of documents on **papyrus** (a reed used for making a material for writing on, which has given us our word 'paper'). The recovery of these documents over the last century or so has given us versions of the Bible earlier than any yet known, fragments of Homer, Plato, Demosthenes and other

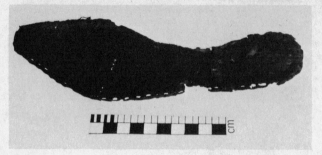

Leather shoe sole from Caerlaverock Castle, Scotland, preserved in the waterlogged moat, where it was lost in the late fifteenth century.

important Greek writers, and everything that is known about ancient Egyptian literature.

Very Wet Conditions

Wet conditions usually cause materials such as bone to disintegrate—two coffins side by side might contain skeletons in totally different states of preservation if one is wet and the other dry.

Coffins that were made in about 1500 B.C. in Denmark have been preserved due to the mounds under which they were buried becoming waterlogged. The water became stagnant in the coffins and the bodies were thus kept in a stable condition. Skin, hair, and ligaments were preserved as well as clothes, ornaments and personal possessions. Wooden sword scabbards, axe handles, birch-bark pails, wooden bowls, and in one case a folding stool covered with an otter's skin, have all been preserved in this way.

Even more remarkable are the remains of the 'bog people', whose bodies were preserved from prehistoric times in the acid stagnant conditions of Scandinavian peat bogs. Under such acid conditions the mineral part of the body was destroyed (p. 31), but hair and skin remained. The

Tollund Man.

fatty substances in bodies can be changed to a fat-wax called **adipocere**. This can happen in less extreme conditions. In 1959, a burial from the Roman period in Britain (A.D. 43–409), was found at Droitwich with part of the brain preserved in a casing of adipocere. The most famous of the Scandinavian bog people is **Tollund Man**, found in Jutland where he had died about 2,000 years ago. Tollund Man's head looks as though he has only recently died, and appears very tanned.

When Tollund Man was found, he was wearing a conical leather cap and had a noose around his neck, suggesting that he had been hanged before being thrown into the bog. This may have been for religious purposes rather than any misdemeanour on his part. The contents of his stomach were so well-preserved that they could be analysed. His last meal was a porridge of vegetables and seeds.

Under the sea, some chemical activities are inhibited, but concretions of shell and sand are constantly laid down. Objects can be cemented together irrevocably, others can be destroyed totally. Sometimes a 'shell' of concretions can be formed around iron objects, preserving their original shape.

Deliberately Preserved Material

Many ancient people (and some not so ancient) have

Section of the Abbot's Way, a corduroy road (made of logs) in Somerset, preserved by waterlogging for at least 5,000 years.

wished to preserve things that would normally perish. The most usual subjects for treatment are human bodies. Sometimes these are preserved for purely religious reasons—the Egyptians, for instance, believed that the body and many worldly goods would be needed in an afterlife. Other people have had a partially practical motive—the Scythians in the first few centuries B.C. were nomads. Their burial rites were only permitted to take place twice a year. Anyone who carelessly died at the wrong time had to be temporarily embalmed while the tribe continued on its travels around the area north of the Black Sea.

Not all embalmers were conscientious—some Egyptians carried out such hurried and careless work that mummies are often damaged so badly when found that the information to be gained from them is slight. Some embalmers faked the mummy—padding it out with bits of wood or even animals! They presumably thought no one would ever discover their bad workmanship.

The process of embalming Egyptian mummies is preserved in pictorial form on many tomb walls. Ancient Indian writings mention the use of honey, curds, ghee (Indian buffalo-milk butter that has been clarified to resemble oil), musk, camphor, saffron, and madder-dyed grave-clothes of silk and flowered muslin.

North American mummies have been found as far apart as Mexico and Alaska. Peru is second only to Egypt for producing large numbers of mummies. In Ecuador, the Jivaro Indians indulged in a specialist form of mummification even in this century—the **tsantsa** or shrunken head. The dead victim's scalp was removed from the skull by a split up the back and peeled off. The skull was then thrown away, the scalp boiled and the slit sewn up. The size was reduced by the repeated insertion of hot sand until about the size of a cricket ball. Such mummified heads have only limited use to the archaeologist since so much tissue is destroyed or discarded.

A more recent example of mummification can be seen in Drogheda Cathedral in Ireland. Here, protected by a glass panel, in a wall niche is the preserved head of St Oliver Plunkett, who was canonised in 1975. Plunkett was a seventeenth-century Irish bishop who was wrongly implicated in the Popish plot and was hanged, drawn and quartered at Tyburn.

Surviving Remains and Mysteries
One murder story that has caused much speculation is the so-called 'Princes in the Tower'. In 1483, Edward V succeeded his father to the English throne at the age of thirteen. After only three months he was deposed in favour of his

uncle Richard, Duke of Gloucester. Tradition said that he
was imprisoned in the Tower of London with his younger
brother and that both boys were murdered at the orders
of Richard III. For years no evidence could be found to
prove that this had happened and many attempts were made
to prove that, even if the crime had taken place, Richard
III was innocent.

In 1674, an urn containing some bones was discovered
in the Tower and was taken to Westminster Abbey on the
orders of Charles II, who believed them to belong to the
two princes. The two skeletons were examined in 1933. It
was found that the ages of the princes corresponded to the
ages of the skeletons at death. The two skeletons had
irregularities which suggested that they were of the same
family. Furthermore, one of the skeletons was badly blood-
stained on the facial bones. This would be expected if death
had occurred by pressure on the face and resultant suffocation. Tradition appears to have been correct that the boys
were murdered by suffocation in the Tower. It is still not
known at whose orders this was carried out, nor indeed do
these facts constitute irrefutable proof.

Another murder story and its possible detection is concealed in a macabre display in Salisbury Museum. A black
rat was found almost perfectly preserved in the head of
William Longspée, Earl of Salisbury, when his tomb was
opened in 1791. The Earl is supposed to have died 'not
without suspicion of poisoning'. The presence of arsenic in
the Earl's body could have accounted for the preservation
of the rat.

4 EXCAVATION

DIGGING, OR EXCAVATION, IS the occupation for which archaeologists are most famous. Without excavation little material would be available for study. Modern excavation is such a specialist undertaking that many archaeologists dig only rarely. One well-organised excavation carried out by professionals produces infinitely more information than many hurried or unprofessional efforts. In many countries excavation is illegal except when undertaken by qualified archaeologists, and it is a great pity that Britain still allows many 'digs' each year which are carried out in the spirit of the early grave robbers and which consequently destroy evidence of the nation's past for ever. For the sake of uncovering local remains or giving the participants a healthy day out, the national heritage is rapidly being decimated almost as fast as the sites in the path of motorways. Any individual or group who contemplates such a selfish action should be strongly discouraged and preferably stopped.

Having started on this discouraging note, it must be said that most professional excavators depend on amateur and volunteer workers whom they train. Excavation, carried out properly, is not only one of the most scientific and complicated aspects of archaeology, it is also the greatest fun.

Once an archaeologist catches a whiff of newly-turned earth, or hears the scraping of trowels, it is difficult to keep him indoors. Most archaeologists continue to take a keen interest in excavation—visiting and advising if not taking an active part in the proceedings—until they are in their bath chairs. The Appendix explains how you can help on an excavation—usually it is as simple as asking if you may.

The Aims of Excavation

The main aim of all properly run excavations is to recover as much information about the site as possible. Everything from the earliest man-made flint tools to the beer glass that was dropped on a picnic last year is treated with equal importance. Even if the excavation has specific aims, the excavator does not dig down at random until he finds what he wants. Excavation is teamwork and the director of a site must be able to call on enough resources or the right experts as they are needed. Many excavations employ experts from other walks of life for short periods—biologists, pollen analysts, doctors or veterinary surgeons, depending on the type of finds.

Excavations are either carried out for research purposes or as 'rescue' operations if a site is threatened with destruction. Research excavations usually have no time limit and are designed to answer certain questions that have been asked by scholars. The site is chosen carefully to produce the maximum information. 'Rescue' excavations are generally carried out under immediate threat and aim at extracting the greatest amount of information in the shortest time possible. If building works are held up, or motorway construction impeded, the costs incurred can be enormous. Much information must be sacrificed in a rescue excavation. The alternative is the loss of everything on the site. There is a great art in choosing exactly how to approach both a rescue site and a research site to gain the maximum results.

How do Archaeologists Know Where to Dig?

Many sites have long stories attached to their discovery but there are a number of ways in which ancient settlements are most commonly discovered.

Rescue Archaeology

Modern building operations often cut through sites which are unknown. The threats are most usual in towns, but open countryside can be subject to quarrying, motorway construction or the laying of field drains, etc., which can reveal remains.

Chance Finds

The presence of large numbers of objects on the surface of the soil can indicate a particular settlement. Roman mosaic **tesserae** (square-cut stones), for instance, could suggest the presence of a villa under the turf.

Surface Marks

As the soil and vegetation cover ruined walls and ditches, bumps and hollows may be all that remain of ancient sites. They show up best in the early evening or early morning when the sun casts long shadows. Snow can exaggerate slight bumps that would otherwise be invisible.

Aerial Photography

More sites are discovered from the air than by any other means. Slight bumps and hollows often show up better from a distance than from ground level. With the aid of

The stone and earth rampart at Mote of Mark, Scotland, which showed up only as a bump in the grass before excavation. Roots in the foreground had to be blowlamped away during the excavation.

stereoscopic photography, the ramparts or ditches can even be viewed in three dimensions.

Crop marks usually show up best from the air. Where walls exist underground plants are unable to put down their roots deeply and grow less strongly and less tall. Where ditches once existed but have become filled in, plants are able to put roots deeply into the well drained humus-rich areas. They thus grow taller and have better colour. The differences in growth show up as a pattern from the air, but are often undetectable from the ground surface. The same phenomenon can be seen by looking at a carpet. The pattern shows up well from the height of a human but is almost indistinguishable from a cat's-eye view.

The right conditions must prevail for crop marks to be noticed. It is possible to fly over an area twice a year for twenty years and miss a site because the lighting and soil conditions are not favourable. Thousands of sites were photographed in the unusually hot summer of 1975 in Britain, many of which had never been seen before.

Placenames

The names of settlements can help in the discovering of sites, although they can be misleading and their study is very complex. Placenames survive long after the settlement they commemorate has disappeared. They tend to become distorted with use and often originated in a different language from that used today. British placenames which sound straightforwardly English can be modernised versions of places named by the Danes, the Anglo-Saxons, the Romans, the Normans or the Iron Age Celts. Archaeological sites are rarely discovered by the use of placenames alone.

Fieldwork

The systematic study and observation of the earth's surface is a vital part of archaeology. Any work that disturbs the soil can reveal finds or sites. Farmers can uncover objects whilst ploughing, building works can cut through walls. The amateur can play an important part in watching such activities and reporting any finds. This can have results that are not only interesting to archaeologists, but can even save life. Old mining shafts, for instance, are currently being searched for officially by aerial photography and other methods, in order to avoid accidents. The large number of fatal and serious accidents caused when people investigate things that are uncovered, however, must impress on anyone interested in archaeology to put safety first. *Never* take chances near open building works, or old mining shafts or any other area that seems to be dangerous. Make your observations from a distance and report any interesting findings to the local museum, archaeologist or university department so the appropriate action can be taken (see Appendix).

What Happens on a Dig?

Long before the excavation starts, the director must
seek permission from the landowner and from the Govern-
ment department concerned if necessary. The regulations
covering excavation vary from country to country and nego-
tiations can stretch out over years.

Finance is the second most important consideration, since
adequate funds must be available to cover the estimated
length of the dig and the tools required. There must also
be enough left over to deal with unexpected contingencies.
Even with the use of volunteer labour for the main working
force, the costs of excavation are staggering. All directors
must be able to keep accounts!

Once these problems have been overcome, the equipment
must be assembled. It is too late to order a hut when the
rain is pouring! Each site will have different requirements,
which may range from a dentist's probe to a bulldozer, and
there is no way of being sure which equipment will be
needed until it is actually about to be used.

The basic requirements for the average dig might be:
spades, shovels, trowels, forks, picks, planks (for wheeling
barrows up the waste or **spoil heap**), kneeling mats, boxes,
brushes (from sweeping to paint brushes), wheelbarrows,
scythes, shears, secateurs, scissors, trays for finds, markers
of various kinds and a host of small equipment such as
pen-knives. Special equipment that might be needed could
range from blow-torches for removing roots of plants, to
pulleys for lifting objects.

Equipment for recording the progress of the dig—paper,
drawing paper, notebooks, pens, inks, pencils, erasers, etc.,
and photographic equipment—is essential. Some elemen-
tary conservation equipment must be available, especially
in remote areas where it might be impossible to rush any

The archaeologist never knows what will turn up next: this fine stone Roman sewer turned up at York, England.

fragile find to a museum, or to call a museum official to the site to treat it. Excavators must be ready for any contingency and must be willing and able to adapt techniques to suit the nature of the discoveries. From the minute the excavation begins the excavator must be ready with pick or brush, trowel or water pump. He or she must be ready to abandon one tool for another, to draw sections, leave areas temporarily undug, to recognise the blue-green stain of decayed bronze and the signs of posts, pits, burning or floors and to treat them accordingly. Although experience will often enable an excavator to predict what he might find, few excavations pass without surprises. As techniques improve, more information can be gleaned from each site.

Before the results of the excavation will be of any use, the site must be surveyed accurately. The various cuttings and areas uncovered must eventually be pinpointed on an official map of the area (in Britain this would be the appropriate Ordnance Survey map). Usually a trained surveyor is needed for this, or someone trained in surveying techniques. A dumpy level or theodolite and other surveying equipment must therefore be available.

A small excavation in Scotland in 1968 at Kirkconnel, Waterbeck.
Notice the turf bank on the right hand side—the spoil was piled
up behind—planks for barrows, and surveyor's white marker
pegs are in position.

The way a site is excavated depends largely on the nature
of the land. A desert site, for example, would be approached
in a very different manner from a waterflooded area. Basic-
ally, the principle is to remove each layer of material in turn,
keeping a record of its relationship to other layers and the
site in general. The topmost layers are removed first. If a
feature such as a post-hole is encountered, it is removed
or treated separately. The way this is done depends on the
site. Some layers such as clay ramparts around forts can
be so hard that nothing less than picks or even mechanical
diggers will remove them. Others are so slight that they must
be removed with teaspoons and paint brushes.

The director of an excavation is responsible for the
organisation, the planning, the interpretation and finally
the publication of the results. He is aided by various assistants who are in charge of the particular areas of the site,
the finds, the photography or any specialist activity such
as collecting pollen samples. The labour force spends its
time on the site or helping the assistants. The only way to

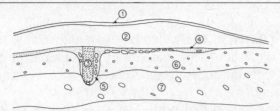

Section through the imaginary excavation cutting from the site described on p. 23.

learn to excavate is to spend years under the direction of a competent excavator (p. 150), and to supplement this experience with learning from books and journals.

Recording

The exact relationship of the layers and the finds must be pinpointed for future reference. A description which merely said, 'the pot-sherd was found in some yellow sand about 10 inches below ground level half way along the trench' would be useless.

Each trench or area is first given a number (trench 4, or area A, let us say). The example shown above is the section through the imaginary site described in Chapter 2 as it might appear in excavation.

Since the last stage reached in the figure on page 23, an additional layer of soil had grown up on the surface and would be removed first (layer 1). This would reveal a dark humus-rich layer which was originally the remains of the thatch, the walls and the fallen posts. On removal of this (layer 2), the archaeologist would encounter a very dark layer of soil stretching almost across the area uncovered. Some stones would be sticking up from its surface (this is the remains of the yard of the house and the cobbles, with domestic refuse amongst them). Before this could be removed, however, a round patch of almost black soil would be seen within the layer. This is the remains of the post which rotted in position (layer 3). This would be removed carefully, leaving a hole the exact shape and size of the original post. The dark soil with stones (layer 4) would then be removed. Further differences would then be revealed around the edge of the excavated post. This is all that is left of the post-hole packing (layer 5). The removal of this layer might well reveal even the spade marks where the man had dug out the post-hole. The next step would be to remove the natural layers, 6 and 7, and the area would be completed.

Most, if not all the deposits except the natural soil of layers 6 and 7 would contain man-made objects. The exact position is recorded carefully. As layer 1 is being removed, any finds from it are placed in a tray marked with the code number of the area or trench, the name of the site (or its initials), and the number of the layer. When that layer has been completely removed, and not before, layer 2 is removed and the finds are placed in a separate tray with the correct code number for layer 2. There will thus be no mistake about where a find was discovered—obviously an important factor since there can be several tons of material from any one excavation, and it is impossible to remember where things came from.

The finds are then taken to a convenient place, in their trays, to be treated. This usually is confined to washing, but some fragile finds need special conservation (see p. 63). All finds that can be marked without causing damage are hand-marked with indian ink with the appropriate code-number from the finds tray. Others are packaged up with labels attached, or in well-marked boxes. The finds assistant keeps a record of every find and where it was found as a cross-check with the finds themselves. If the director wishes

The 1975 excavations at the Roman town of Cirencester (Corinium) showing many features and layers in process of excavation. The white labels in the side of the excavation record the layers already removed. Notice the mutilated mosaic pavement still in position in the middle foreground.

to know what came from a particular layer, he or she simply has to refer to the code book for the finds.

On site the records show the depth of each layer, its nature and content, as well as any miscellaneous information and measurements. Photographs, drawings of the sections and plans are made at frequent intervals.

When the dig has finished the director prepares the final report for publication. He or she analyses and researches the finds, compares them with those from other excavations and finally makes an interpretation of the site. This process can take years—far longer than the excavation itself.

The example we have just described is, of course, grossly simplified to illustrate how the archaeologist sets about interpreting what is found in the soil. It is highly unlikely that such a simple sequence would ever be encountered. The layers we have distinguished would almost certainly be divisible into many more and the excavation process would inevitably be more complex.

The system of coding material used in the example is not necessarily to be found on all excavations. Some sites have almost no stratification, others have many strata and few finds. Sometimes material is found in large quantities that requires separate coding—masonry blocks or wallpainting fragments, or pieces of mosaics, perhaps.

Different Types of Excavation

Area excavation involves removing a large area totally to establish the plan of features dug into or resting on the natural ground surface. Such a technique is only possible when there are few layers to interpret. It would merely destroy evidence in areas such as towns where there is a large build-up of layers.

Grid excavation is usually employed when there are many layers on a site. It involves laying out a grid of squares or 'boxes' with unexcavated areas or **baulks** in between them. Each box is excavated separately and a complete record can be kept by watching and drawing the **sections** (sides) of each wall of the box. If a layer or structure appears in more than one box, the baulks can be removed separately and the boxes amalgamated.

Trial trenching is used when the archaeologist only wants to find out particular information about the structure he is investigating, such as how long it is, what happens at the corners, or whether it conforms with other known examples. By this method narrow trenches are dug in the areas most likely to answer the questions.

A story circulates amongst British archaeologists about

a director who put down a cutting across a Roman fort
to find out its dimensions. Roman forts are so standardised
that it is often possible to calculate the type of force they
housed simply by knowing the size. The cutting uncovered
one side of the fort and was extended to find the other side.
The cutting grew longer and longer. It reached the point
where the wall was expected and continued. Eventually it
was so long that the fort seemed to be the largest ever found.
The excavator stopped the digging. A second trial trench
was put down at a different angle. The wall was found where
it had originally been expected. The original cutting had
been placed inadvertently through a gateway which was
slightly out of the normal position. Archaeology is always
full of surprises!

Some sites need special treatment. **Round barrows** (burial
mounds) are usually divided into **quadrants**. Waterlogged
sites need pumps and shuttering to protect the workers.

5 OBJECTS AND MUSEUMS

NOWADAYS, BUSES AND CARS pass through the little village of Thatcham in Berkshire with little thought for the past. But 10,000 years ago, before the houses were built and the roads tarmacked, the inhabitants lived in a camp. They had to catch their food and make their own entertainments. One day, probably when out on a hunting expedition, one of these **Mesolithic** (Middle Stone Age) people found a piece of stone of extraordinary shape and brought it back to the camp to show his family and friends. It was a flint. Unlike most natural flints it appeared to have been chipped and worked to form a cutting edge. They pondered over it, discussed its origins, wondered if it had been made by one of their forgotten ancestors. But they were unable to make any sense of it, because in the eighth millennium B.C. there was no way of telling how old an object was or whether it was man-made or natural. All they could do was keep it at the camp, the object of many camp fire discussions and arguments, and there it stayed until it was uncovered by archaeologists in 1960.

People have always been fascinated by things from the past. One of the first true collectors was the princess Bel Shalti-Nannar of Ur in Mesopotamia, who set aside a room in her house for the display of ancient Sumerian artefacts.

Many Romans were interested in old things, but by far the most devoted collectors were the Italians and other Europeans in the fifteenth century and later, who, at the time of the Renaissance, made collections of beautiful ancient objects to adorn their houses. People were looking back to the classical past of Greece and Rome and wishing their times were as great. They seemed to think that by displaying a bust of some ancient Roman emperor some of the greatness and glory of the times would rub off on to their own lives. They were interested almost entirely in the beautiful objects the past had left, and their collections were called museums or 'temples of the Muses' (the Muses were Greek and Roman goddesses who looked after the arts).

It was from these early collections that the study of objects from the past has developed. As science developed in the nineteenth century, objects that had been dug up began to make more sense. Instead of arguing about the function or age, people could apply scientific methods to find the truth.

The seventeenth-century idea about the origins of flint tools was given by Aldrovandrus, who said they were: 'Due to an admixture of a certain exhalation of thunder and lightning with metallic matter chiefly in dark clouds which is coagulated by the circumfused moisture and conglutinated into a mass (like flour and water) and subsequently indurated by heat (like a brick).'

However wild the first guesses may have been, curiosity had been stimulated. As time has passed, museums have started to house all ancient objects, from the most beautiful to the most ugly. The purpose is less to marvel at beauty and art than to study the objects in order to find out about the past. Accordingly, museums today can have geological and natural history specimens as well as archaeological. Archaeological museums can be as large as hundreds of

View across the Acton Scott farmyard, Salop, showing cart, henhouse in foreground and fine thatched pigsty in background.

acres. They can have exhibits ranging from cottages to railway engines. They can be tiny rooms cramped with Victoriana or huge halls containing totem poles and shrunken human heads. It is in museums that most objects discovered on archaeological excavations eventually end up.

One of the most exciting new museums is at Acton Scott in Shropshire. This working museum is intended to demonstrate life on a Shropshire farm before the advent of the petrol engine or electricity. The first full farming year was 1976, using breeds of animals that were to be found on Shropshire farms before 1900. When visited by the authors in the previous season of 1975, the farmyard was littered with gaily painted carts, other carts in process of restoration, and badly neglected iron farming implements waiting to be restored to full working order. The implements that had been restored were collected in one room of the renovated farm buildings. A cheese press is inscribed: *'T. CORBETT'S PRESSES HAVE GAINED FOURTEEN FIRST PRIZES*

A plough suitable for hard land. It could turn a furrow 14 in.
wide and 9 in. deep.

ALL COMPETED FOR'. A root cutter bears the adver-
tisement *'UNCHOKABLE'*. Rare facts of history are
recorded on these almost forgotten implements. G.
Llewellyn and Sons were responsible, for example, for the
manufacture in Haverfordwest of an end-over-end churn.

The principal implements required for a mixed husbandry
farm before 1900 are as follows:

1. Cart—1 horse
2. Waggon
3. Liquid manure cart
4. Clod crusher
5. Iron roller
6. Horse-hoe
7. Drill harrow and
   grubbers
8. Ploughs
9. Double mould-board
   plougher
10. Light grass harrows and
    chain harrows
11. Heavy seed harrows
12. Three-horse grubber
    and scarifier
13. Corn drill
14. Grass seed-sowing
    machine
15. Drag harrows
16. Turnip-scuffer
17. Turnip drill and clod
    crusher
18. Mower and reaper
19. Sheaf binder
20. Horse-rake
21. Tedder
22. Horse-fork or elevator
23. Potato-raiser
24. Threshing machine
25. Chaff cutter
26. Turnip cutter

A Tamworth pig at Acton Scott museum.

27. Winnowing machine   29. Oil cake breaker
28. Oat bruiser or mill-
      stones

Many of these objects are so obsolete as to be unrecognisable to modern farmers. The days when winnowing machines were needed are long since past. Electricity and petrol were the main factors in changing these methods.

The Acton Scott Museum is a living museum in a real sense. Careful back breeding has produced such rarities as the pig opposite, a noisy porker whose grunts and squeaks called the authors through a field of Roman geese to see him. This pig was produced by first breeding a Tamworth (above) which is a rare Shropshire type, with a wild boar. The offspring were themselves mated, producing *philodendron*, a specimen as similar to the kind of pig that roamed Britain in the Iron Age as it is possible at present to achieve.

Philodendron, an iron age pig.

Nowadays, museums are very different from the collections of dusty cases in dark rooms that they used to be. Instead of being miscellaneous collections of unusable old objects they are more easily enjoyed and understood. The museum at Cirencester, for instance, is a splendid example of modern layout. Roman objects are not merely on display, they are shown in the kind of context in which they would have been used. A model of a Roman lady stands in a reconstructed dining room; a low table with fruit in front of a couch which would not be out of place in many homes can be seen on an original mosaic floor. A Roman kitchen complete with oven and griddle for cooking food in the shiny pots can be seen nearby. Typical herbs used in Roman cookery have been collected from the courtyard garden of the museum.

Behind the Scenes

This is where most of the work in museums is carried out. Although most museum cases look full, there is usually a much larger body of material in back rooms. Box after box of pottery or iron from excavations, from chance finds, or collections that have been given in the past, are analysed and examined, coded and deciphered. Scholars spend time comparing objects, trying to work out when they were made, how or by whom.

One of the first methods used by the nineteenth-century archaeologists for analysing objects was **typology**. This was a method of looking at objects, invented by a Swede, Oscar Montelius, who studied a series of railway carriages and pointed out that it was easy to arrange them in the order in which they had been made because the later they were the more complicated they were.

This is true of many things—an obvious example would be cars: with a bit of thought almost anyone would be able to say that a car made in 1908 was made earlier than one made in 1976. The later one would be faster, safer, more economical and more comfortable. It would not be reasonable to suppose that as people continued to make cars they would make them less comfortable and less safe. Over the years objects tend to develop and become modified until they have reached perfection (**functional stasis**). Very few objects reach this stage, as man's capacity for making improvements is almost unlimited. An excellent example is a pair of shears or scissors. Iron Age shears are not very different from those we use today. It is therefore very rarely possible on typological grounds alone to tell the age of these objects.

The working out of a typology in the first place is complicated, and consists of comparing many thousands of objects and finding out exactly what contexts they came from, to see if they were associated with any objects of known date. One of the best examples is the Roman pottery called **samian ware**. This very distinctive and beautiful pottery was made in factories in the first two centuries A.D. As fashions changed, so the shapes of samian and the decoration on the pots changed. The potters tended to stamp their names or initials on the pots, and in many cases details of their working lives have been found out from other sources. As a result, any pieces of pottery made by certain potters can be dated fairly closely wherever they are found.

One of the breakthroughs in the study of this pottery came in the excavation of Pompeii. The eruption of Vesuvius is known to have occurred in A.D. 79. Amongst the finds were unopened cases of pottery ready for sale in the shops. The particular type and style of pottery was thus proved to have been made in or just before A.D. 79. All other similar pieces found in the Roman Empire can be assumed to have been made at around the same date.

It is from such painstaking comparison and analysis of tons of material over the last century and a half that it is possible for apparently undistinguished finds to be assigned unerringly by archaeologists to a particular time or area.

One interesting habit that humans have, which is often useful to archaeologists, is of copying obsolete fashions in modern materials. The Anglo-Saxons, for instance, built stone churches in the seventh century and later. The original churches were almost certainly built of timber, like Saxon houses, but conservatism, as well as the need to strengthen the walls, led to the stone churches being built to resemble the timber. Strips of stone (**pilasters**) were built into the walls in place of the timbers in the original buildings (p. 62). Such copies which no longer have any

Bradford-on-Avon, Wiltshire. An Anglo-Saxon church with pilaster strips on the walls, which may be skeuomorphic copies of older timber churches which have not survived.

function except decoration are called **skeuomorphs**. They are used sometimes by archaeologists to find out what earlier versions which may not have survived may have looked like. Skeuomorphic decorations can be seen frequently in modern clothes fashions—shoe buckles, for instance, which have no use in fastening shoes.

Conservation

One of the most important functions of a museum is the repairing or restoring of objects that are badly damaged. The finds of the Sutton Hoo ship burial (p. 26) have been reconstructed by the British Museum at least twice as technology and knowledge have improved. Fragments of the helmet when excavated, for instance, covered three trestle tables. A number of problems were posed by the first reconstruction. It was not understood, for example, why the

Sutton Hoo Helmet—the original reconstruction by Mr Herbert Maryon.

Sutton Hoo helmet—new reconstruction after recent discoveries.

helmet gave such good protection on top but almost none to the vulnerable area of the cheeks and neck. The second reconstruction afforded greater protection, so the problems no longer existed.

Some Methods of Treatment

Many objects require specialist treatment either when found or within a few days of discovery. Temporary measures are often carried out at excavations, but the bulk of conservation work is done in museums.

Objects that are flaking cannot be lifted and therefore need consolidation. This can be done by painting or spraying them with a suitable consolidant that can be dissolved at a later stage without harming the object. In some cases the object can be partly or totally immersed.

If an object falls to pieces on being lifted from its find spot, reinforcement must be applied. Small objects can be coated with a suitable consolidant wrapped round with strips of bandage and kept in place with some suitable tacky substance. Once this has dried the object can be lifted, and the consolidant dissolved. Larger objects are more difficult to move and often special methods have to be invented to suit the particular problems.

Pottery restoration is about the only form of archaeological restoration that can be practised in everyday life. It is relatively easy to restore a pot if none of the pieces are missing. The most suitable glue needed is HMG or UHU, and other equipment will include a tray of sand, Sellotape, or masking tape, and possibly some string or a clothes peg. The pot is first fitted together in a 'dummy run' to make sure in which order the pieces must be fitted together. It is only too easy to stick a pot together and then find that a small piece has been left out and cannot be inserted because of the angle of the breaks.

The pot should be stuck together starting from the base and working up to the rim. The glued pieces of pot should be held together until dry with tape or a clothes peg, and propped carefully in a tray of sand. The process should be slow—only two or three pieces should be stuck together at any one time, and no more should be added until the glued pieces are dry.

Plaster of paris is the best substance for filling in the gaps. A suitable piece of plasticine is rolled flat until it is slightly larger than the gap to be filled. It is then dampened slightly to encourage it to stick to the pot and pressed down behind the gap. The edges of the pot should be dampened too at this stage to help the plaster to adhere to the broken sides. The pot itself should be protected from accidents with the

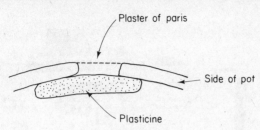

Restoring a pot of which only a piece is missing.

runny plaster by masking tape or Sellotape. The plaster should be mixed until fairly runny, then poured into the gap or worked in with a spatula. It must be remembered that plaster of paris dries very quickly. Any plaster that inadvertently spills on the pot should be removed immediately. When the plaster has hardened, the plasticine is removed and the plaster smoothed down with glass paper. The restored part can then be painted to resemble the rest of the pot.

Restoring a pot that has more than a few pieces missing is too complicated to be attempted without considerable practice.

Wood must be kept damp if it was wet on discovery. If allowed to dry out it might disintegrate entirely. If found on an excavation it is normally placed in plastic or polythene bags after being sprayed with a mixture of 1 per cent fungicide to 99 per cent water.

Some finds require special treatment and the ingenuity of the conservator is called on. Several tile and pottery kilns have been lifted in Britain and taken to museums.

The methods of removing mosaic floors from their find spots have been perfected over the years. The mosaic is covered with glue or synthetic resin and sacking is placed

Fragments of wall plaster found at Lullingstone, Kent, can be compared with more complete Roman wall paintings and reconstructed into a frieze.

over it. When the resin has dried, boards are placed on the top to keep the mosaic rigid, and the entire floor or large sections of it is removed complete with mortar backing. The boards and sacking are removed by dissolving the resin and the mosaic can be relaid. Another, more satisfactory, method involves taking the tesserae alone without the mortar backing. The adhesive material is placed in position over the top of the mosaic, which is then rolled up as though it were turf.

Museums carry out a great deal of reconstruction work from fragments that are found. Wallpaintings, for instance, can often be reconstructed in their entirety if only a few pieces survive, by comparison with other better preserved examples.

6 HOW OLD IS IT?— DATING THE PAST

Historical Dating Methods

What have A.H. 28, A.U.C. 1403, and 9 got in common? They are all ways of referring to the year A.D. 650. The first is a Mohammedan date meaning *Anno Hegirae* 28 (Latin for 'in the year of the Hegira'). The Hegira is the era which started when Mohammed escaped from Mecca to Medina (traditionally in A.D. 622). The second is a Roman date: A.U.C. stands for *ab urbe condita* or *anno urbis conditae*, which is Latin for 'from the founding of the city'. It refers to the traditional date when Rome was founded (753 B.C.). The third date is one which would have been used by people living in the Byzantine Empire (which was based on modern Istanbul) and refers to the ninth year of the reign of the emperor Constantine III, who began ruling in A.D. 641.

One of the most important requirements of any organised society is a method of counting the years. It was relatively easy for ancient man to work out that there were roughly 365 days a year and to make the necessary adjustments, but it was much more difficult to distinguish one year from the next. One man might remember a particular year as that in which he obtained his first herd of cattle or moved into his new house, while another might remember it as the year in which he lost all his crops in the rain. The more com-

Sumerian foundation cone, probably from Lagash. These cones
were placed in the foundations of temples, and recorded the
name of the builder from which the date can be worked out. This
cone has lost its name and is thus of uncertain date, possibly
about 2200 B.C.

plicated the society, the more important is the system of
dates. Nowadays, it is imperative to keep an eye on the date
to know if the car insurance needs renewal or when the
school holidays begin. Governments need to keep a check
on the date to know when taxes were paid or laws came
into effect.

Most societies have thus devised systems of dating which
were based on occurrences that were important to society
in general, rather than to individuals. The Egyptians
counted the years with reference to the yearly flooding of
the Nile and many peoples have used the length of their
rulers' reigns. In some cases it is possible to correlate
different date systems. At the time when Egypt was occupied

by the Romans, two sets of dates occur in the records—the Roman and the Egyptian—for the same events. From this overlap period it is possible to work backwards and find out the Roman date for events that are only recorded in Egyptian records.

The most common system of dating in the world today is calculated from the traditional date of the birth of Christ. Hence the letters 'A.D.', which stand for *Anno Domini*, the Latin for 'in the year of Our Lord', and B.C., meaning 'before Christ'. Events recorded in the Bible and elsewhere are also to be found in some Roman writings. Thus from the correlation of Roman, Egyptian and biblical dating systems, it is possible to put dates to events that happened in ancient Egypt, into terms that are readily understandable today.

Dates are not always written on paper or papyrus—some useful dates for the archaeologist can be written on buildings themselves. Buildings of known date can then be compared with buildings of unknown date. This is especially true of buildings that were put up in the Roman period or after A.D. 1500 in Britain. The Romans tended to put an inscription above their public buildings which mentioned the year and month of the building operation and who was responsible for the work. At Speke Hall in Liverpool an inscription above the door records that:

THIS WORKE 25 YARDS LONG WAS WHOLLY BUILT BY
EDW:N:ESG: ANO 1598

This means that the approach to the house (not the house itself) was built in A.D. 1598. From the available documentary evidence it is possible to identify EDW:N as Edward Norris, who lived at Speke Hall from 1568 to 1606.

Dates can thus be fairly accurately worked out for

Inscription at Speke Hall, Liverpool.

societies which had systems of writing. However, no evidence of writing was found dating from before about 3000 B.C., after which most civilised societies kept records. Many less complicated societies had no need for writing, or even for counting the years, except as an aid to farming. Yet archaeologists can often state very firmly when certain peoples built particular settlements or moved from one area to another.

Dates have been found for such prehistoric peoples by using known historical evidence and archaeological finds. Until the late nineteenth century, when scientific methods of dating became possible, archaeologists had to rely entirely on finding objects whose dates of manufacture they knew, in the same context as objects of unknown date. If, for example, a grave was found to contain a dagger, an axe and a spear of unknown date, and a faience bead (a type of glass and paste) exactly similar to some made in Egypt in the sixteenth century B.C., it would be reasonable to assume that the other objects in the grave were of approximately the same date. Other axes, spears or daggers of the same type found in other contexts, but without the datable bead, could likewise be assumed to have been made at around the same time.

Using this system and typology (page 60), links were built up between civilised areas which had written records, and prehistoric Europe.

The chief problem with such a method is that some types of objects were in constant use for a long time. Artefacts found in graves, for instance, might have been heirlooms and several hundred years old when buried. This is especially true in the case of things that had been traded from other areas, which were highly prized. At the end of the chain of dates the system can be several thousands of years wrong. Even so, the method has proved surprisingly accurate in the light of more scientific dating methods.

Stratigraphical Dating

The stratigraphical sequence on an excavation is vital for putting dates to the buildings.

In the example taken in Chapter 4, layer 1 was obviously laid down after layer 2. Layer 2 could not possibly have been 'inserted' in some way afterwards. Similarly, the post-hole (layers 3 and 5) was dug after the natural layers 6 and 7 were put down since it was cut into them. The post-hole was also obviously dug before layers 1 and 2 came into existence. It can also be seen that the post-hole (layer 5) and packing were put in position before the layer of domestic rubbish and cobbles since these cover it. The cobbles do not cover the inner part (layer 3), which was all that remained of the rotten post, since the post rose up to take the walls of the house.

It is possible to work backwards in a series of logical

steps and to work out what happened in which order on the site.

It is usually possible to determine the age of a site from the finds in the layers. Suppose, for instance, that the man, while digging the post-hole, had broken a beaker from which he had been taking refreshment. If he had swept the pieces into the hole for further packing, or even if one piece had fallen in by mistake, the pottery would be found by archaeologists in layer 5 (p. 49). Since the post would, in this instance, have been placed over the sherds and rotted in position, there would be no possibility that the pottery had arrived in that position at any later date. By comparing the pottery with pieces of known date and origin, it would be possible to state when the beaker had been made and thus, roughly, when it had been broken, since pottery rarely remains unbroken in everyday use for many years. An approximate date for the construction of the hut could then be inferred. Pottery is very useful for dating because of its short life.

Coins might seem a better way of finding dates since they normally have some information on them that can pinpoint their exact date of manufacture. Unfortunately for archaeologists, coins were often kept in circulation in the past for hundreds of years. All that the presence of a coin might indicate is the date *before which* the layer could not have been put down; this is called the *terminus post quem*. Sometimes it is possible to give a date *after which* a layer could not have been laid down: the *terminus ante quem*. This might happen, for example, if a floor was known to have been laid down in a particular year. Anything under the floor would have a *terminus ante quem* of the year when the floor was laid down.

In excavations, layers or features can often be given both

a *terminus post quem* and a *terminus ante quem*. Within the two dates it might be impossible to be more precise.

It is for this reason that archaeologists are more likely to use phrases that sound very long-winded instead of definite dates. In Chapter 1, the writer of the poem the *Ruin* was referred to as living in the eighth century. This was not because the authors could not be bothered to look up more precise dates, but because it is not possible with the present state of knowledge to state exactly when, within the period A.D. 700–800, the poem was written. Such phrases as 'in the early part of the third quarter of the first century A.D.', meaning between A.D. 50 and 60, are common in archaeological writings.

It is possible for objects to be moved from one layer to another in the soil. The archaeologist must know when to make allowances for such disturbances and when he can be certain that the finds are in their original position. The topmost layer of most sites will be disturbed by the traffic of animals and humans, for instance. Any find at this level could be of great significance, but is equally likely to have arrived there by any one of an unlimited number of ways.

Since the nineteenth century several other methods of dating events in the past have been invented. They require complex scientific techniques and are used together with stratigraphy and history. Some of these methods are described in the following chapter.

7 SCIENCE AND ARCHAEOLOGY

THE TWENTIETH CENTURY HAS
seen the development of many scientific techniques which
are now widely used by archaeologists in many areas of
research. Archaeology itself is rapidly becoming a science
in its own right.

Radio-carbon Dating

At the end of World War II the discovery of a method
of dating organic material (such as wood, charcoal and
bone) by measuring the radio-carbon content revolutionised
archaeology.

When plants are alive they absorb carbon dioxide from
the atmosphere. Some of this—the radio-carbon isotope
carbon 14—is slightly radioactive. Animals who eat plants
absorb some of this radioactivity too. When the plant or
animal dies the carbon-14 starts to decay at a fixed rate.
After about 5,568 years, only half the radioactivity is left.
(The figure for the **half-life** of radio-carbon has been
adjusted a number of times in the recent past as inaccuracies
have been found. At the time of writing the exact figure
is 5,730 $\pm$ 40 years, but the figure normally used in
the calculations is still 5,568—archaeologists have to
make own adjustments.) By measuring the amount of

radioactivity that remains it is possible to arrive at a date when the organism died.

As might be imagined, radio-carbon dates are not accurate to within very short periods, and many factors can disturb their accuracy. It is necessary, for example, to keep any sample for which a radio-carbon date is needed out of contact of all organic material—even windblown cigarette ash.

Most dates are given with a margin of possible error which is expressed as plus or minus so many years. A date from a prehistoric site might look like this: 1,957 ± 150 B.P. (B.P. stands for 'before the present day'). This means that the date is somewhere between 2,107 and 1,807 years before the present day. A further confusion is that the present day is taken for this purpose as 1950! Put into more recognisable terms, therefore, the date 1,957 ± 150 B.P. means somewhere between 157 B.C. and A.D. 143. Most excavators try to have several radio-carbon dates to make sure that contamination has not taken place. Radio-carbon dates only refer to the year of death—a wooden post, for instance, might have been cut from the tree many years before it was used for building.

Dendrochronology
This method of dating is based on counting tree-rings and has recently been used to prove that for some periods radio-carbon dates are inaccurate by hundreds of years. As a result, archaeologists have had to make many adjustments to their theories and ideas of prehistory. It is commonly known that the age of a tree can be worked out by counting the rings around the stump. It is not so well known that the rings are not all the same thickness, but vary according to the environment. More important still is that these varia-

tions are governed not simply by local conditions but by conditions that prevail over the entire northern hemisphere. This means that trees from North America can be correlated with trees in Western Europe and dates can be linked. Trees planted in the same year, for instance, will have an identical ring pattern—perhaps two thick rings followed by three thin, and so on. The rings do not have to be the same thickness (that varies with the species of tree), but the *proportions* are similar.

Some trees live to great ages, so it is possible to work out links far back into prehistory. In Britain the oak can live up to 500 years, and in North America the bristlecone pine can live for over 1,000 years.

Fixed dates in the tree-ring link are usually found from old beams in houses of which the building date is known. Dendrochronology is a very precise method of dating wooden material such as beams or posts in houses.

Potassium-Argon Dating

Potassium-argon is used for dating very remote periods. It can only be used on igneous or volcanic rocks, and is not widely used by archaeologists. The earliest dates for the first men have been arrived at through this method.

The way potassium-argon dating works lies in the fact that once the volcanic lava hardens into rock, the radioactive potassium it contains gradually changes into the gas **argon** and is trapped inside the rock. When the rock is heated to melting point, the gas is released and can be measured. The potassium still present in the rock can also be measured. The older the rock, the more argon it will contain and the less potassium.

When excavations were carried out in Olduvai Gorge in East Africa by Dr Louis Leakey, the fossil remains of the earliest men were found in a layer of mud sandwiched between two layers of igneous rock. By dating each rock layer, Dr Leakey was able to date the layer of mud in between, and thus date the fossils it contained.

Archaeomagnetism

If the pointer of a compass is released it will immediately point to the magnetic North Pole. This point changes slightly as time passes, though not sufficiently to be noticed in normal everyday life. The same principle is used in a method of dating called archaeomagnetism, or **remnant magnetic dating**. Any objects made of fired clay, such as hearths, can be dated by this method.

Igneous rocks and fired clays contain oxides of iron which make them slightly magnetic. When heated, the rock or clay loses its magnetism but regains it on cooling (for instance, when the firing process on pottery has been completed). The regained magnetism is directly related to the intensity and direction of the earth's magnetism at the time of cooling. The magnetism of a pot or hearth is thus 'locked' into the time and place of cooling and can be measured. A hearth made in A.D. 1600, for example, will be distinguishable from one made in A.D. 1900. Archaeomagnetism is a complicated process and has the drawback that the position of the pottery object must be pinpointed with a degree of accuracy not possible in normal excavation.

Thermoluminescence

Many minerals which are found in the clays from which pottery is made emit light because they have absorbed radiation. The absorption of radiation starts when the pottery is fired. By measuring the amount of light being emitted, it is possible to reach a date for the manufacture of the pottery. The pieces of pottery must not be exposed to sunlight for more than a few minutes or they will absorb too much contemporary radiation. A sample of the surrounding soil must be taken for comparison.

Pollen Analysis

One of the most indestructible substances is pollen. When viewed under the microscope it can reveal what plants were growing in the past, so that a total picture of the environment around particular sites can be built up. Pollen is usually preserved best in waterlogged layers on archaeological sites.

Insects and Snails

The shells of snails and some parts of insects, such as the wing cases of beetles, are often well preserved. It is often possible to discover what type of environment surrounded a site from studying the particular types of insects—some flourish in damp forest conditions, others in open cultivated fields, for instance. Changes in the environment over the years can thus be studied.

Bones

The types of animals that lived near sites, which were domesticated or which were hunted for food, pose some of the questions that can be answered from the study of animal bones. The customs of animal farming—whether the animals were killed when young, which cuts of meat were favoured, which animals were popular, whether domestic pets were kept—can throw light on past societies.

Human bones from burials can reveal at what age the individuals died, and from what diseases they suffered. A study of the bones of medieval monks found in the excavations at Winchester Cathedral showed that many suffered from arthritis. This crippling bone disease is aggravated by damp conditions to which the monks must have been accustomed, living in unheated buildings. Other bones from monasteries (for instance, Norton Priory, Cheshire) revealed a remarkably high percentage of lead. It is thought that this was absorbed through the use of pewter in drinking vessels. This is an example of how an apparent luxury (most people in the Middle Ages could not afford pewter) was in fact a disadvantage.

In 1827, a tomb in Durham was opened which was thought to be the grave of the early medieval saint, Cuthbert. He had been described by the Venerable Bede as walking with a limp. When doctors examined the body (which was remarkably well preserved), they found that it had indeed belonged to a crippled man, and thus provided supporting evidence that the tomb was indeed that of the Saint.

Parasites
These little organisms often have a remarkably long duration and point to the many ills ancient people suffered. As early as 1910, the eggs of the parasite *Shistosoma haematobium* were found in the kidneys of two Egyptian mummies. In 1954 the eggs of the roundworm, and cysts from the parasite *Entamoeba* were found in the frozen body of an Inca child in the Andes. Liver fluke has been discovered in soil layers in a Slav settlement in Poland.

Teeth
Dental surveys have been carried out on the teeth of ancient peoples. It has been discovered that dental decay increased when men started eating cereals. This coincided with the discovery of farming. The increased carbohydrate

in the diet meant less healthy teeth. Some people, including the first farmers and the Anglo-Saxons, were unable to prepare their food well. They had to grind their corn down in querns made of rough stone—grit broke off into the flour in such large quantities that teeth were worn down rapidly.

Not only people with a fairly primitive way of life were prone to bad teeth. The Romans had the skill and the time to prepare and eat splendid feasts. Eventually they ate three meals a day, of which the least elaborate was breakfast. This consisted of bread, honey and dried fruits—all high in sugar and carbohydrate content and very bad for teeth. The Romans had the skill to remove teeth, however, and many old Romans ended up with no teeth at all.

Ultra-Violet Radiation

The excavation of bones has led to the use of ultra-violet radiation in archaeology. If a skeleton is exposed to adverse conditions it may become stained and indistinguishable from the surrounding soil. The excavator might thus do more damage than good while trying to uncover it. If the bones are badly stained and broken, it might be impossible to gain any useful information, such as the size or shape, which is necessary to determine sex or age.

Some substances (including bone) can absorb ultra-violet light radiation which is not visible to the naked eye. The substances then emit wavelengths of light, some of which are visible. This is called fluorescence, and is in common use in clothing and signs. The fluorescence usually emitted by human bone is creamy in colour, but is purple if the bone is stained by the soil. If a fluorescent lamp is directed on to a badly stained skeleton, the bones will be distinguishable from the surrounding soil and the excavator will be able to remove the soil and take photographs and measurements. The bones have to be cleaned with a knife, never a brush.

Remarkable detective work has been carried out using fluorescence. A Bronze Age cist burial had been disturbed by farm workers before archaeologists arrived at the site. The skull had been removed and then replaced. When the cist was excavated some bones were found to be disarticulated. It was thus imperative to find out the exact position of the skull when discovered to find out whether the man had been decapitated. A fluorescent light was applied. The areas of skull which had been in contact with the soil showed up as purple, the rest as creamy fluorescence. It was thus possible to determine the exact position of the skull in the grave. The head had been articulated with the body.

Regional Studies

Scientists can discover where substances were made and thus which areas had trade links with which. By studying prehistoric stone axes, geologists were able to pinpoint the source of stone in many cases. Axes made in north Welsh factories were traded as far afield as Scotland. The study of clays has led to the knowledge that certain types of pottery used in Britain in the sixth century A.D. were in fact made in France. The alloys that make up bronze objects can show where the ores were found.

Computers

Computers have been invaluable in sorting out material that is too cumbersome for rapid analysis. One of the most spectacular analyses by computer was made at Karnak in Egypt. Tens of thousands of blocks of stone were discovered, most of which had fragments of scenes showing Queen Nefertiti. Under the direction of an American, Ray

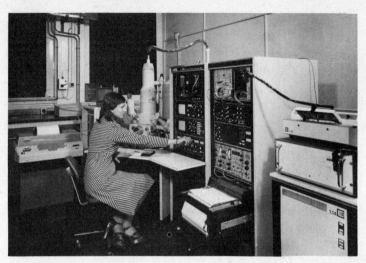

An electron-probe microanalyser at Liverpool University being used for research on Dark Age metals.

Smith, the stones were recorded in a computer and the scenes were reconstructed. The stones showed amongst other things that the queen was of much greater importance at court than was previously thought.

Metallurgy

Sometimes the study of ancient metals by metallurgists can have surprising results. Metal from the excavations at the Mote of Mark (p. 145) was analysed by the metallurgy department of Liverpool University. What appeared to be a minute fragment of gold was in fact mostly phosphorus, though it could still be considered as gold. What appeared to be silver, was pure iron oxide. A corroded iron bar (p. 31) turned out to be a blade which had been hardened and had had so much carbon added that parts were steel. The production of steel was not known to have been possible in the Dark Ages. Furthermore, the blade appeared to have been deliberately formed into steel, and not just a freak. An iron wedge was proved to be a lump of iron which someone had started to fashion into a blade, possibly the first process in making a sword.

These are just a few of the techniques used in the study of the past. With the use of new techniques, information can be gleaned from the smallest piece of pottery or sample of soil, enabling important discoveries to be made from apparently very flimsy evidence. As the occasion or problem demands, further scientific techniques will certainly be utilised in the future.

8 EXPERIMENTAL ARCHAEOLOGY

TWO MEN FACED EACH OTHER in the field of combat, each carrying a sword and a round shield. A sword flashed and struck and one of the shields was almost cut in two.

This was no fight between ancient warriors, but a controlled experiment into Bronze Age warfare carried out by Dr John Coles of Cambridge University. The experimenters had been curious about the large numbers of weapons that were made in Europe during the Bronze Age. The period after about 900 B.C. seems to have been violent, to judge by the spears and shields, swords and body armour that were produced. Most of the shields that have survived were made of thin beaten bronze, but one example, found in an Irish peat bog in 1908, was of leather.

The only way to find out whether bronze was more efficient than leather was by experiment. The leather shield had obviously not been made of rawhide: it would not have survived in a peat bog, nor would it have lasted its owner long in the wet Irish climate. A sample of the leather was analysed and the shield was found to have been made with a tanning process using natural vegetable tanning agents. But how had it been moulded into shape? Two wooden moulds for making similar shields have been found in Ireland. Using copies of these, experiments were carried out to find the best way to harden leather, to make it waterproof and to mould it into shape. The most effective method was found to be to dip the leather in a bath of hot water (80°C) for thirty seconds and then to beat it into the mould. A replica of a bronze shield was also produced, as nearly similar to Bronze Age examples as possible.

The stage was set for a battle using the replica shields and genuine Bronze Age swords and a spear. The spear punctured the bronze shield with a stroke and the sword cut it almost in two. In contrast, the spear barely punctured the leather, and after fifteen savage blows with the sword the leather shield had only a few cuts on its surface. Neither combatant was hurt.

From the experiment it was deduced that the bronze shields found were used for ornamental purposes: on parades, perhaps, or as offerings to the gods.

Many experiments have been made on a variety of ancient remains to find out how they were made or how they were used. The results, as in the case of the shields, have not always turned out to be what was expected.

If you were stranded on an island with no pots or pans, how would you heat water for cooking, for instance? The cooking would be limited to roasting on hot stones unless some means of containing water could be devised. Several experiments have been carried out with boiling water to find out how ancient man managed. A book published in 1581 by Derricke, shows a picture of four stakes in the ground with an animal skin between them and a fire underneath. The skin was being used as a 'pot'. An account of the Scots' retreat from the English in 1327 describes how there were 'more than 400 cauldrons made of hide with the hair

Cooking in a skin.

left on full of meat and water over the fire to boil' at the Scottish camp.

This all sounds very straightforward. But when experiments were made in 1966 by Dr Michael Ryder, the results were not encouraging.

Dr Ryder put four iron stakes in the ground and suspended a sheepskin over them tied with string at the corners. The use of iron made the experiment easier, though it was realised that if ancient man had been able to make iron stakes, he would almost certainly also have used metal cooking vessels. The sheepskin was found to contain about a gallon of water which was about three inches deep in the deepest part. After 15 minutes the water had reached 40°C but needed much stoking of the fire. After an hour, the heat reached 45°C (well below the 100°C needed for boiling point) and the skin had shrunk so much that another stake, this time made of wood, was used to shore it up. A mutton shank was added at this point. A great deal of water leaked out, and in the end the wooden stake burned through, leaving us to wonder what would have happened if all the stakes had been of wood. Eventually the experimenters had to abandon the dinner, since it was obvious that the shank would never cook by this method. The meat was eaten and enjoyed by a sheepdog.

Three years later Dr Ryder repeated the cooking experiment, this time using a paunch instead of a skin for the cooking vessel. Less water could be heated, but a greater heat was achieved, although the paunch was badly affected by the fire. It was concluded that a more effective method would have been to use hot stones in the water ('pot-boilers').

In 1954, Michael O'Kelly made a cooking experiment using hot stones which was so successful that the experimenters were able to enjoy a well-cooked meal of mutton. Professor O'Kelly had found a series of post-holes, a stone slab, heaps of charcoal and stone and a wooden trough at a site he had been excavating in Ballyvourney, Ireland. He concluded that this was a Bronze Age cooking place, but could not be sure until the structure had been tried out.

The trough was 1·8 m. by 1·0 m. by 0·4 m. deep and was partly sunk into the ground. On each side the heaps of stone and charcoal were interpreted as hearths, and were used in the experiment. The trough was filled with water, and hot stones from the hearths were dropped in. After only half an hour the water began to boil and was kept at boiling point by the occasional addition of further hot stones. A leg of mutton, wrapped in straw to keep it clean, was added and cooked for 3 hours 40 minutes, and then eaten.

Experiments of a more ambitious nature have been carried out. In the nineteenth century, General Pitt Rivers, one of the greatest early archaeologists, tried to find out how the original diggers had used the bone implements he had discovered in the mine shafts at a flint mine at Cissbury, Sussex. He found it was quicker to use his bare hands than the shoulder blade shovels.

A similar experiment was carried out in 1960 at Overton Down, Wiltshire. In order to find out how long ancient man took to build burial mounds (some of the most common remains in Europe), and also to find out the effect of the weather on the earthworks, an artificial mound was constructed using only ancient types of tools. It was hoped that when a similar mound was excavated, comparisons could be made with the artificial mound and some answers to common problems could be found. The location of the experimental mound was similar to that of many earthworks in southern Britain. During the experiment no modern tools were used—shed red deer antlers from Woburn Safari Park were used first, but were discarded in the end in favour of modern wapiti antlers, since wapiti are nearer the size of ancient deer than modern red deer are. The antlers were then used, as prehistoric man had used them, to hammer and prise the chalk out, and proved to be very strong tools. The loose material was then transported by using wicker baskets. These were very difficult to carry; it was found that the only efficient method was on the head.

None of the modern diggers were adept enough to use this method. Shovels in prehistoric times seem to have been the scapulae (shoulder blades) of cows, or horses. The experimenters accordingly used horse scapulae. They managed to obtain the scapula of a small Indian elephant, too—this did not prove such a popular tool. The experimenters found that the scapulae were very good for scraping, but such bad shovels that they were led to the conclusion that ancient diggers must have had another,

Silbury Hill, Wiltshire.

probably wooden, implement for shovelling, that has not yet been found in excavation.

The experimenters were timed carefully and it was found that ancient tools were three or four times less efficient than modern ones, and much slower to use. From the timing experiments it was possible to work out that the average Bronze Age burial mound in Britain required the work of six or eight men for two weeks. To dig out the ditch around one of the biggest and most famous of monuments, Avebury Circle, would have taken at least a hundred men a year and ten months working ten hours a day. Including the time taken for tipping the loose material, the whole operation could have taken as long as nine years. It must be borne in mind, however, that these figures could be inaccurate simply because the modern diggers were not used to digging with bone implements. Prehistoric man may have been much quicker. Silbury Hill, the largest man-made mound in Europe, which is near Avebury in Wiltshire and was excavated for the BBC during 1969–70, and is still of unknown function, would have taken at least 50 million basket loads to construct. Whatever the reason for its construction, it must have been a good one!

Without such experiments, it is difficult to get any idea of how the mounds might have been constructed.

One of the very first 'experiments' in archaeology was carried out in the last century when the Vicomte Lepic used a polished Stone Age axe to cut down a tree to judge how efficient it was. The result of this and other experiments was that although the ancient axes were efficient in cutting down trees, they were not so efficient as modern methods. Allowance must always be made, however, for the fact that the experimenters will be unskilled in using ancient tools, will probably be less used to physical labour than their ancient forebears, and will certainly have less motivation.

Gordon Childe, the famous prehistorian, believed in trying to make replicas of things using what he believed to be the techniques of ancient man. He built and fired a rampart near Finavon in Angus to see whether it was possible to make the stones melt from the heat if he used wood to build a framework for the wall. He found he was able to melt them, and thus proved that the lumps of molten stone which he had found in his excavations at Finavon had probably been melted by the timber frame of the rampart which had been accidentally fired.

For centuries men have wondered just what effort was needed to erect Stonehenge. In the 1950s Professor Atkinson of Cardiff decided to find out by trying to transport a replica of one of the bluestones of Stonehenge, which weighed just under two tons, by the methods he imagined would have been used. He believed the stones would have been transported on rafts along waterways wherever possible, and he discovered that once the stone was loaded with a crane on wooden planks laid across three canoes, it took only four schoolboys to pole it up a river. Not only that, but he found that it drew so little water it could have been transported up shallow creeks and streams.

For land transport Professor Atkinson tried sledges— these were rolled along on log rollers, as the builders of Stonehenge would not have known about the wheel. He found it took 12 men to drag the two-ton stone on its sledge, and he required another team of 12 to collect the rollers and put them in front of the sledge as it moved forwards. Without rollers far more men were needed. It took 32 schoolboys to drag the stone and sledge over firm ground and up a slight slope. The large stones of which Stonehenge was constructed weighed about 40 tons each, and were brought from 32 kilometres away, which would mean a team of about 880 men to pull a stone one kilometre a day. It was reckoned that to have erected the main circle would have taken perhaps 1,500 men five years.

Similar experiments showed that it took 180 men to raise one of the upright stones into position once it was on the site, using shearlegs. If this seems to be a great deal of man power, it pales into insignificance compared to experiments that were carried out on the building of the Mayan ritual centre at Uxmal in Mexico. A staggering 7·5 million man-days was calculated as necessary for the operation. One result of these experiments is that even the most daunting engineering feats are shown to have been possible with only simple equipment if enough man-power could be called upon.

More recently, a similar experiment was carried out on the site of the Roman fort at the Lunt near Birmingham,

Reconstruction of a gateway at the Lunt Roman fort near Birmingham. Part of the granary can be seen through the gate.

Warwickshire. When the site had been excavated it was found that the fort had been occupied in the middle of the first century A.D., a time when the Romans were building many forts with great speed in Britain. In 1966 the experimental rebuilding was started. With the help of labour from a prison in Leicester, 11 m of rampart was constructed from turf and infilled with soil. It was not known exactly how high the rampart had been originally, but the width was known. Since there must have been a walk along the top of about 2 m wide, the angle of the slope of the walls and the approximate height (3·6 m) could be calculated. The distance from the top of the rampart to the bottom of the ditch that ran around the fort was thus 4·3 m—a daunting prospect for any prospective attacker.

The experimenters cut the turf to the specified Roman sizes of 1·5 by 1·0 by 0·5 Roman feet (44·4 by 29·6 by 14·8 cm). The turfs each weighed about 32 kg and required two men to place them on the shoulders of a third for

The reconstruction of Hadrian's Wall at Vindolanda (Chesterholm), Northumbria.

efficient transportation to the rampart, where they were
placed turf to turf, earth to earth in two banks. The centre
of the two turf banks was infilled with earth from the ditch.
The turf was cut with saws and crescent-shaped blades which
are known to have been used by the Romans. In order
to build this first stretch of rampart, between 5,500 and
5,750 turfs were used, and 7–10 men working a 6-hour day
finished the job in 20 days. It was estimated that the entire
fort of the Lunt could have been put up by its force of
300 men in about 9–12 days.

From this experiment it was possible to calculate the
length of time needed to put up larger forts such as that
at Chester, which housed a legion of about 5,000 men. Half
the force could have built the fortress in about 12–14 days.

One of the most ambitious feats the Romans achieved
in Britain was the building of a turf wall across the low-
lands of Scotland (the Antonine Wall)—a distance of 59 km.
The wall was about 4 m wide and could have been built
by 6,000 men in about 100 days, although other troops
would have been needed to build temporary housing and
to feed the workers.

The rebuilding of the Lunt has not been abandoned at

A reconstructed Celtic iron age chariot made by the BBC. Chariots like this were used against Julius Caesar when he invaded Britain in 55 and 54 B.C. (Copyright BBC.)

a stretch of 11 m. By now a gateway has been added in timber. This was designed from Roman military data and from representations on Trajan's column in Rome. It took 25 Royal Engineers three days to construct. A granary was built inside the fort. Granaries were constructed slightly differently from most Roman buildings, since their floors were raised from the ground surface to avoid damp.

At Roman **Vindolanda** (Chesterholm), the reconstruction of a further Roman building feat has been carried out in recent years. A stretch of the wall that ran across from Carlisle to Newcastle (**Hadrian's Wall**) has been erected, complete with a turret and ditch outside.

On a less spectacular scale, excavators of the Saxon town of Thetford, Norfolk, in 1967 found vessels that must have been used for drinking beer just before the Norman conquest (A.D. 1066). Detailed research was carried out, in the interests of science, into the drinking habits of the Saxons.

Because of the pronounced lip on the rim of the beer mugs, it was concluded that the Saxons were very messy drinkers!

Experiments on how ancient man built his ships, or houses, how he engaged in warfare, how he conducted his everyday life, have frequently shown us that things were not always as they might appear at first sight, and will continue to help us to understand the problems that people had and how they overcame them.

9 UNDERWATER ARCHAEOLOGY

PARADOXICALLY, UNDER-
water archaeology owes its existence to a fire. Around 1820 a fire broke out at a farm at Whitstable, Kent, and rapidly spread from some haystacks to the stables. Pails of water were used without success to put out the flames. At length, one of the bystanders, John Deane, borrowed the helmet from a suit of armour at the farmhouse and put it on his head. He ran a pipe from the helmet to an old, dry pump in the farmyard and the farmer began to pump air into the helmet. Using this private air supply Deane was able to enter the stable through the dense smoke and lead the horses to safety. This episode gave him the idea for a diving helmet, and he experimented until he had devised a helmet suitable for taking underwater. With the aid of this he explored the wreck of the *Royal George* which had sunk in 1782. He also invented a watertight rubber suit.

The *Royal George* was only the first of a series of wrecks investigated by Deane, which included the sixteenth-century *Mary Rose*.

During the nineteenth century many improvements were made to diving equipment, and research was carried out on particular wrecks and the finds recovered from them. During this century the aqualung was invented and the

development of skin diving has greatly eased the examin-
ation of wrecks. Nevertheless, very little interest in wrecks
or submerged sites was shown by archaeologists until after
World War II, and the exploration of wrecks was confined to
looting expeditions no better than those of the nineteenth-
century antiquaries who broke into the pyramids, destroying information. Unfortunately, 'archaeological' investigations are being carried out even today with no other object
than to recover as much treasure as possible. Details about
the finds could easily be recorded at the same time.

Underwater archaeology today is concerned with the
study of wrecked ships and their contents, and the excavation of sites which were once on dry land, but which have
become submerged for some natural reason such as a rise
in sea level.

The value of wrecks in the study of the past is inestimable.
Each is like a miniature world under the sea, for the underwater archaeologist can be certain that everything on board
was in use at exactly the same point in time. In the case
of the wrecks of ships which are known from history, such
as the Armada wrecks, one can be certain not only of the
year in which the objects were in use, but even of the month
and the day. One can also be fairly certain that the objects
recovered represent a reasonable selection of those in use
at the time, in contrast to the finds from a land excavation
which often represent the rubbish that people were no longer
interested in.

It is very rare of course for perishable materials to survive under water for a very long time, and the sea can often
eat away metal much faster than acids in the soil. Now and
again, however, 'freak' conditions can occur under the sea.
This was the case with the *Wasa*, sunk in Stockholm
harbour in the year 1628 on her maiden voyage and re-

The *Wasa*, 1628. The *Wasa* had a displacement of just over 1,300 tons. Her beam was some 38 ft. and her draught a little more than 16 ft. Drawing by Nils Strödberg based mainly on Sam Svensson's reconstruction suggestions.

covered in 1961 and refloated. The *Wasa* had completely filled up with mud which preserved her contents. When the 700 tons of mud were removed from her decks, finds included a sea chest containing the personal belongings of a sailor, including a fine broad-brimmed felt hat. Some skeletons were found on board, complete with their clothes and purses filled with coins.

Usually the tides spread the remains of the ships and their cargoes over a very wide area, only the ballast stones remaining in one place, or perhaps the cannon. It is rare for the timbers of the ships to survive intact, but when they do they tell the archaeologist a lot about methods of ship-building. The objects on board are usually covered with concretions from the sea, and these sometimes preserve the objects inside them, though the task of removing the often rock-hard deposits is slow and painstaking.

The *Wasa* in 1961—the ship was mounted on a concrete pontoon in the framework of the aluminium building that now houses her.

The lower gundeck of the *Wasa* after excavation, looking towards the bow. The mud has been removed from the ship. Along the starboard side a gun carriage is lashed in front of each gunport. The huge horizontal beam in the background is the bit around which the anchor cable was lashed.

The excavation of sites under water is similar to the excavation of sites on land. Here, however, the remains are not buried under layers of soil but under the deposits on the sea bed. Everything has to be carefully plotted and photographed and the remains carefully revealed using special techniques devised to cope with underwater conditions. It is not possible to use a pick and shovel under water, as each shovelful would be swept up by the swell and just make the water cloudy. Instead, a gadget rather like a giant vacuum cleaner is often used.

Some of the first scientific excavations of wrecks were carried out in the Mediterranean. An American archaeologist, George Bass, who was an expert on Bronze Age Greece, was sent out in 1958 to examine a Bronze Age wreck at Gelidonya, off the coast of Turkey. He had never dived before, nor had many of his team, but under the guidance of an expert diver he mastered the basic skills needed for an aqualung and launched an excavation using exactly the same methods that he would have used on land. Unfortunately, the wreck had been lying so long on the sea bed, that the sediment had formed rock-like concretions which had bound the cargo (which consisted of bronze ingots) to the rock. To tackle this problem, Mr Bass photographed, mapped and labelled all the shapes that concealed the cargo. He then chipped the concretions into 200–300 lb. lumps and raised them to the surface, where they were pieced together using the code on the labels. Work then went on 'excavating' the remains on dry land and gradually the concretions were chipped away to reveal the fragments of ship and cargo, the tools and some of the belongings of the sailors.

When the excavation was finished the boat could be seen to date from the time that the *Odyssey* was written by

Homer. Where wood had been trapped under the cargo and protected from the oxygen in the sea water it was well-preserved—among the perishable finds was a wicker basket.

Mr Bass then turned his attention to the wreck of a Byzantine ship off the Turkish coast near Yassi Ada, which was much better preserved. Although no record of its loss existed it was possible to state, from the coins that were found, that it went down in the seventh century A.D. (the coins were dated between A.D. 610 and 641, so the wreck must have occurred sometime after A.D. 641). From this wreck it was possible to recognise a rectangular mound of amphorae—storage jars for wine—which had been the main cargo, a mass of what appeared to be anchors at one end, and some smaller amphorae and tiles at the other; hence Mr Bass was able to work out which part was the bow and which the cargo hold and the crew's quarters.

Everything was recorded carefully before any attempts were made to lift the material. Although bronze is often well-preserved under the sea, iron corrodes away to nothing. Before this happens, however, algae and sediment usually coat the metal with a 'fur' and chemical reactions form a shell which remains when the metal has disappeared. Mr Bass collected the hollow concretions which he had carefully plotted and used them as moulds to cast plaster replicas of the long-vanished objects. So careful was his excavation that the original appearance of the ship could be reconstructed. The task was made easier by the preservation of part of the wooden hull, of which each fragment was carefully drawn. Among the numerous finds from the ship was a bronze balance for weighing cargo. It carried on it the name in Greek of the captain—George Senior.

Nearer home, exciting discoveries were made during the investigation of the *Girona*, a Spanish Armada vessel sunk off the coast of Northern Ireland in July 1588. The wreck was located in June 1967 by the nautical archaeologist Robert Stenuit, and a meticulous excavation carried out: 6,000 hours of diving were spent on the wreck. Throughout the investigation the conservation laboratory of the Archaeology Department in Belfast University and the Ulster Museum were kept busy on the finds. There were nearly 10,000 of these, ranging from gold and silver coins, lapis lazuli cameos of Roman emperors (set in gold), fragments of silver dishes, a gold salamander set with rubies, a gold cross which was traceable to the *Girona*'s captain, to sherds of pottery. A gold ring, inscribed 'Madame de Champagney, 1524', was traced through patient research in old documents to its original owner—it had been given to a Don Thomas Perrenoto, who was recorded as having gone down with the *Girona*. Almost as exciting as the jewels were the nautical instruments which shed light on navigation in the time of the Armada, and the first Armada cannon ever recovered, as well as 11 breech blocks (some still containing their powder), and 200 stone cannon balls.

10 MAKING SENSE OF THE CLUES

THERE ARE TWO SIDES TO archaeology—the research and the interpretation. The first part of this book has explained how the clues to the past are gathered, the rest will show some of the ways in which those clues have been interpreted.

Some 2,500 years ago in the area of France that is now the little village of Vix, a great funeral was in progress. The most important lady in the Celtic tribe who lived in the area was dead. Her family was rich and powerful. They gathered together all the fine goods she had used in her lifetime—her wagon, her bronze bowls, her silver bowl and gold diadem, her brooches. The prize piece was a vast bronze vessel for mixing wine that had been imported from Greece, filled with Greek wine to grace the barbarian feasts they all loved. It was almost as high as a man, and is the only one of its kind to survive in the world—even in the area of its manufacture mixing bowls like this are only known from smaller examples in pottery. The Princess of Vix, as she is now known, was pampered and revered; even in death her followers and family gave her only the best. The treasures that were placed in her grave can only have been a fraction of those they possessed and used every day.

This is a tragic and romantic little story that was un-covered by archaeologists in the snowy winter of 1953. Since then scholars have set to work on the finds, compared them with other objects, discussed them, made tests on them, interpreted them and reinterpreted them. How had a Greek mixing bowl and a painted Greek drinking cup reached this remote tribe? Had they been diplomatic gifts from Greeks anxious to trade with the Celts? Was there other evidence for such a trade, and what did it suggest? What did the grave tell us about the burial customs and beliefs of the sixth-century B.C. Celts? As a result of the discovery a great deal is now known about the people who lived in the neighbourhood of Vix in the time of the princess, about the way of life she must have led, and about how they might have thought.

But has this any real importance beyond the curiosity of a pretty story? At a time when man has reached the moon, can trap the rays of the sun to heat his houses, can transplant heart and kidneys from one person to another, can defend his property with radiation beams and travel by air, what relevance has the story of the Princess of Vix?

People have always looked to the past to find the answers to present problems and to try to avoid future difficulties. Despite floods, volcanic eruptions, inflation, deflation, plagues and famines, mankind has not only survived, but has developed.

A study of the past can help us to understand the present. It is not always easy to see, for instance, why people should co-operate with others if there is no direct benefit to them-selves. The results of people not co-operating with each other can be seen over and over again in the past. Until mankind co-operated to engage in farming, for instance, all spare energies had to be put into hunting and simply staying alive. Once there was surplus food, people had time to develop ideas. Within a thousand years or so of this co-operation men began to co-operate even further and to live in towns. The path was set which led to the space-age. Men have developed in the past 10,000 years infinitely further than in the preceding four million years.

From studying the past we can learn to evaluate our own society—to discard things that are detrimental, to improve others or to adhere to those which cannot be improved on at present. A simple example that occupies people nowadays would be the role of women in society. Women in the past have sometimes enjoyed the highest positions of power, or have been treated equally with men, or have been treated as slaves; obviously the lady in the Vix burial was regarded as important by the society in which she lived.

How Archaeology Developed

A study of the way archaeology itself developed can help us to understand why some people still wrongly imagine that an archaeologist is an old white-haired man who digs up treasures in some hot climate. This picture is a legacy from the first colourful characters who became interested in the remains of the past. Their methods and ideals are almost all out of date or out of favour by now.

The first important developments in the study of the remains of past societies came in Italy during the Renaissance. The princes who ordered their followers to dig up treasures to adorn their palaces were not archaeologists, but dilettantes who were interested only in works of art. Although archaeology would almost certainly not have developed without these men, they also did a great deal of harm in destroying evidence as they hacked through layer after layer of remains to reach their objectives.

This enthusiasm for the remains of the past very rapidly spread to Western Europe. But whereas the ancestors of the Italians had been the civilised Romans, the French and British had no such glorious past. Instead, they tried to romanticise about the barbarians who had been living in their countries around the time of the Romans. The French became very interested in the ancient Gauls, the Celtic people who fought against Caesar, while the British became passionately interested in the ancient Britons. At this time the idea of scientifically collecting and comparing information had not yet been developed, and so the early antiquaries, as they are called, had to speculate about the remains from the past and often weaved fantastic stories to explain them. Some of their inventions have survived to this day—the idea of the Phoenicians coming to Britain, the idea that Stonehenge was built by the Druids, and the stories of the Lost Tribes of Israel and Joseph of Arimethea's visit to Britain all were made fashionable around this time.

Some of the early antiquaries began trying to record accurately what they saw, even though they did not understand what they were recording. **William Camden** (1551–1623) was one of these, and travelled around looking at local remains and customs—his survey of Hadrian's Wall was stopped due to the hostility of the wild northern English!

The tradition started by people like Camden continued until the eighteenth century, when the greatest exponent was **William Stukeley** (1687–1765). Stukeley was typical of the early antiquaries. He was a rich man with plenty of time to devote to his interest and a lively mind. He was told by his doctor that he should travel in the countryside to cure his gout, and to give himself an interest on his travels he started recording ancient remains. On one occasion he noticed a Roman road swerved round the base of a prehistoric mound to avoid it, and from this he correctly deduced that the mound was older than the road. Such a deduction might seem obvious to us now, but it was a novelty in the eighteenth century, and was to lead to many of the developments described in this book.

Stukeley was fascinated by Stonehenge and by the Druids, and used to dress up as a Druid (or his idea of one) and hold Druid parties in London.

All the early antiquaries were unable to overcome one great problem. Because there were no written records for prehistory, they had no means of telling which prehistoric sites were oldest, or which objects were made later than which. Because a churchman, Bishop Ussher, had worked out from the Bible that the world was created in 4004 B.C., they had a mere 4,004 years in which to fit everything that was probably earlier than the time of Christ.

It was not until the nineteenth century that the obstacle was overcome, and people began to see how the remains of prehistory fitted together to tell a story. The break-through came when in 1816 a young Dane, **Christian Thomsen**, was given the task of trying to arrange the material in Copenhagen Museum into some kind of order. Looking at all the objects, it appeared that there was a time in the past when people used only copper and bronze for their tools, not iron, and before that a time when only stone tools were used. From this he deduced that before metal was discovered men used stone tools, and then used bronze until the discovery of iron. This led to the invention of the **Three Age System**—the recognition of a Stone, Bronze and Iron Age—which is still used today as a convenient method of dividing up the prehistoric past.

The three ages, however, still had to be condensed into the short period of time from 4004 B.C., the supposed date of the Creation. Geologists, not antiquarians, were the first to prove that the world was very much older than 6,000 years. A stone axe had been found in the seventeenth century at Gray's Inn Lane in London with the bones of extinct animals, and since then people had wondered about how old mankind was. The publication of books about geology and fossils, followed by Darwin's *The Origin of Species*, which was published in 1859, opened men's minds to the idea of the great antiquity of Man.

In the same year that Darwin's famous book was published, stone tools were discovered by **Boucher de Perthes** under the gravels of the Somme. Several other instances of what appeared to be man-made objects under geological strata were greeted with disbelief. The Bible, after all, stated that God had made the earth on one day and Man on another. No provision had been made for the possibility that part of the world had been made before Man, and another part afterwards. One suggestion even went so far as to state that God had placed the flints under the geological strata at the Creation in order to trap men into the sin of reason. Reason told people that the flints must be older than the geological formations, but belief in God forbade them to indulge in reason. Nowadays very few people agree that reason is a sin, but in the eighteenth and early nineteenth centuries the development of science as well as archaeology was severely hindered by such strong beliefs. Once these problems had been overcome, the study developed rapidly.

While some antiquarians were collecting and arguing over objects, others were busy digging. Until the nineteenth century excavation had been pure vandalism as people dug to try to find treasures. Squads of labourers were employed to find ancient objects for the personal enjoyment of their employers.

The first attempts at describing objectively the circumstances in which objects were found were made by **Sir
Richard Colt Hoare** and **William Cunnington** in 1812. 'We
speak from facts not theory,' wrote Sir Richard in the introduction to his account of the excavations near Stonehenge.
But in spite of his good intentions, he lapsed into romanti-
cism and wrote about a skull which 'grinned horribly
a ghastly smile'. Meanwhile, in Egypt, a circus strongman
turned archaeologist, Giovanni Belzoni, was looting tombs
with happy abandon. 'Every step I took,' he wrote later,
'I crushed a mummy in some part or other.'

It was not until the end of the nineteenth century that
scientific excavations came into being. The inventor of
modern excavation techniques was **General William Pitt
Rivers** (1827–1900). Pitt Rivers first became interested in
the past through studying the development of the rifle. After
his military career, he organised his excavations like a military campaign. At his own expense he began excavating sites
of all periods in Cranborne Chase, and published the
results in four large volumes, *Excavations in Cranborne
Chase*, in which everything he had noticed was recorded,
whether it made sense to him or not. So precise were his
records that modern archaeologists have been able to re-
interpret his findings and to identify features that were unsuspected from the state of knowledge in the nineteenth
century.

Archaeology had come of age, although Pitt Rivers' techniques were not taken up immediately. It was not until after
World War I that Sir Mortimer Wheeler made improvements to Pitt Rivers' methods. Improvements have been
carried out ever since and will continue to be made.

As archaeology has developed, so the answers people have

expected it to provide have changed. How they interpreted the clues that they uncovered depended partly on how much they already knew and the development of science, but mostly on the questions they asked.

One of the most famous ancient monuments in Britain is Stonehenge in Wiltshire. This mighty prehistoric stone circle has attracted people throughout the ages, if we can judge by the presence of finds from almost every period since its construction. Stonehenge as it is today, was put up about 4,000 years ago in the Bronze Age, but Iron Age pottery sherds, fine Roman pottery called samian ware (see p. 61), some Saxon coins and a belt ornament, some medieval arrowheads and a wine bottle which probably was lost during William Cunnington's excavations there in 1801, are testimony of the site's attraction at other times.

By the seventeenth century, interest in Roman civilisation had spread to northern Europe. Stonehenge was thus attributed to the Romans. In the following century people began to rebel against the cold logic of the Romans and tried to escape into a more romantic world of magic and mystery. British people became more interested in the ancient Britons, and in particular the Druids. Although these priests certainly existed in Iron Age Britain, they were not the wild romantic figures they were reputed to be in the eighteenth century. Stonehenge was then admired for its mysterious element and supposed to have been built by the Druids.

The romantic view of Stonehenge was fostered even into this century. The way in which the monument has been viewed more recently has varied according to the interests of the day. Scientists have been absorbed in recent decades with the problems of space exploration, with the result that Stonehenge has been seen as a prehistoric observatory.

More recently, with the development of computers, the Bronze Age monument has been declared to be a primitive computer. Today's archaeologists are most interested in what the past tells us about the structure of society. Stonehenge has thus been used to find out how society was ordered in the Bronze Age.

As already mentioned, the answers people get depend on the questions they ask. This is not to say that the past can 'prove anything'. We can ask questions, but we will not necessarily come up with the answers we wanted or were expecting. The essence of archaeology is to see what the answers are, not to expect particular answers.

When you visit museums or ancient remains you should always try to find out what they have to tell you by asking yourself questions about them, rather than relying entirely on the facts in guidebooks. Nothing is more boring than a string of facts and dimensions. Some of the most tedious hours the authors have ever spent in their lives were passed in their youth in museums and at ancient sites. Instead of asking themselves questions and trying to answer them, they simply gazed blankly at labels that said inexplicably things like 'Middle Minoan III, Rhyton', and went away perplexed!

There are four questions the archaeologist must ask himself initially about any site or find—*Who made (or built) it?*, *When was it made?*, *Why was it made?* and *How was it made?* Great archaeologists have always been able to ask the right questions in addition to these, but if we can answer these four, we are well on the way to understanding the people who used or lived in the remains.

Who Made it?
Fortunately for archaeologists, human beings are very

conservative. People become used to a particular way of life and seldom see reason for change. Even in this decade when fashions have changed in developed countries faster than ever before, people are surprisingly slow to take advantage of new techniques or ideas. Houses, for instance, are still normally built with straight walls and sloping roofs, although the materials and techniques exist that could produce much more adventurous shapes and furniture to fit. Clothes are still made of wool or linen and even man-made fibres are carefully fashioned to resemble natural materials.

People are also unwilling to appear too different from their neighbours. National and regional customs and preferences are quickly built up. If you were given photographs of the buildings and their contents, it would be easy to state that an Eskimo household belonged to people with a very different way of life from a North American or British household. But how would the American and British households compare with each other? Each might contain a fridge, a car, a garden and similar standards of living. A short period of research into other American and British households would reveal subtle differences between the two. America, Britain and Greenland belong to three different **cultures**.

In the past, people have been even more conservative. If there was a tradition that particular types of decoration were used on pottery or clothing, the makers saw little reason to change. Analysis and research has enabled archaeologists to work out which characteristics belong to which peoples.

If the names of the people do not exist (as for example in the prehistoric period), archaeologists have to invent names to help them to refer to different groups. Usually, the name chosen roughly describes the characteristics which distinguishes one group of people from their neighbours.

Hence some prehistoric people who lived in Britain and the Continent are called the Beaker people because of a particular type of beaker they used that was not favoured by their neighbours.

Who Built it?

Buildings can be as informative as objects. Who erected buildings is determined partly by the distinguishing features of the buildings themselves (as with Roman forts and villas, Greek temples or Iron Age hillforts), partly by the finds and partly by the date of the construction. For relatively recent periods it is often possible to compare the remains found in excavation with standing examples. When prehistoric buildings are discovered the finds, characteristics of the site and the buildings are grouped and analysed in the same way that objects are.

When Was it Made or Built?

This question is answered in a variety of ways which have already been described in Chapters 6 and 7.

Why Was it Made?

If we can find out why an object was made or a building erected, we can understand the problems or the skills of the owners. Objects can tell us, for instance, whether people had to defend themselves against their enemies and how efficiently they did so. The Romans, for instance, possessed weapons that many less advanced societies were not able to produce. Whilst their foes, the European barbarian Celts, fought with swords, the Romans could bring catapults capable of projecting large stones into the battle field. They devised such gadgets as caltrops—spiked iron objects which were placed in the enemy path to maim horses.

The Minoans in Crete, about 1,500 years before, were also organised civilised peoples, but when they made weapons they did so for ritual purposes, not war. Their requirements obviously differed from those of the Romans.

One find can have enormous repercussions and give us a disproportionate amount of information. Sir Mortimer Wheeler once found a sherd of pottery in Madras Museum in India. It had originally been found in Pondicherry, about 80 miles to the south, and by asking the question 'Why was it found there?' he opened up a new chapter in archaeology. Sir Mortimer went in haste to Pondicherry and found there three or four museum cases deep in dust in an inner room of the public library. Wiping away the dust with his arm he saw more fragments of Roman storage jars, part of a Roman lamp, a Roman intaglio and a number of Indian objects. An excavation was carried out at the site where the objects had been found, and the Roman trading post at Arikamedu, the name of the site at Pondicherry, was discovered. The Romans were now known to have traded as far afield as India.

Why Was it Built?

The answer to this question is extremely revealing. As with objects, the function of a building can show us the ingenious (and often bizarre, to modern thinking) ways in which people overcame their problems. We can find out from buildings what sort of life the builders led, which occupations they considered important. From this we can ask ourselves why they were able (or forced) to lead such lives. The richer Romans, for example, built fine dining-rooms and elaborate bath buildings. They had the resources and the political stability to enjoy luxuries. The Vikings, to take a random example, lived a much more spartan way of life. Even the richest Viking household tended to house the cattle under the same roof as the family. This method afforded greater warmth in the bleak northern climate.

The plans of buildings can show us what type of society was common. The Minoan palace at Knossos, Crete, for instance, was extensive and rambling (p. 124). The king lived in a royal suite, but many other people lived in the same building in other apartments. An Iron Age chieftain in southern Britain, however, would have lived in a separate hut from his followers within the ramparts of a hillfort.

The finds can prove important in determining the function of a building. Domestic refuse such as sherds of pottery or glass fragments suggest that the building was a house, not a cattleshed. A burnt patch of clay or stone in the centre of a building points to a domestic hearth. Conversely, the absence of domestic remains suggest that the building might have been, for example, for housing animals, or for religious purposes (such as a temple).

How Was it Made?

The technological skill of people in the past is an important pointer to how they lived. The differences between a civilised organised society and a more primitive people are easily illustrated by the way they made their everyday objects. Simply the pottery-making can illustrate this— while most prehistoric peoples made clumsy hand-made pottery or used leather or wooden vessels, more sophisticated societies used a potter's wheel and mass-produced pots.

How Was it Built?

The answer to this question can show how advanced the builders were technologically. The ancient Egyptians built pyramids for their dead kings and officials. Their skill was infinitely greater than that of the prehistoric people living in Europe at the same time who were unable to cut and dress the stone.

General Inferences

Sometimes it is possible to infer facts from the absence of a commodity, though this can be misleading. One of the few cases where this is possible concerns *Australopithecus*— one of the ancestors of man, who lived in Africa. No evidence of fire has been found in or near the homes of *Australopithecus*. Although it is *possible* that they knew about fire, it is unlikely.

Simply because an object is not found, does not mean it was not made. Clothing does not exist for many periods of the past, but we must not infer that people went around naked. The survival of toggles, for instance, shows that skin clothes were worn, the survival of buttons points to the use of wool or linen.

11 ARCHAEOLOGY AND WELL-KNOWN SOCIETIES

Pompeii—A Roman City

IT WAS FEBRUARY 5, A.D. 62. The slopes of Vesuvius, the high mountain overlooking the bay of Naples, were covered with vines and fertile fields. The land had gained its fertility from the addition to the soil of lava from an ancient volcanic eruption that had separated the islands of Capri and Ischia from the mainland. In A.D. 62 no one alive could remember such remote geological events and the people seemed as safe as anywhere else in Italy.

A huge roar rent the air. The Pompeians thought it must be the god Jupiter giving vent to his wrath. The sea began to heave in the harbour and they thought that Neptune, the god of the sea, was angry too. Then the pavements began to crack, the columns of the houses and public buildings began to shake and the Pompeians and all the inhabitants of the other towns and villages on the slopes of Vesuvius realised the truth. The volcanic mountain was about to erupt.

Even those who managed to reach the country were beset by dangers from the chasms which opened up without warning on the mountain slopes. The reservoir near the Porto Vesuvio (one of the main gates of Pompeii) burst and flowed into the city. Quake after quake continued into the evening

Cast of a body from the Roman city of Pompeii.

until at last the mountain was quiet and the people could return to clear up the mass of fallen and still falling pillars, the ruined drainage system and the collapsing houses.

But it was not this catastrophe that led to Pompeii and the neighbouring towns of Stabiae and Herculaneum and others being preserved for posterity.

The real horror and devastation that led, paradoxically, to their preservation, occurred 17 years later when the volcano once more erupted and poured lava and pumice on to the mountain slopes without respite. The devastation of A.D. 79 was so complete that the floods and damage of the previous eruption seemed insignificant.

After the quakes of A.D. 62 the Pompeians had rebuilt their city lavishly. They continued their steadily prosperous way of life.

The warning the Pompeians should have taken came in August, when the earth shook and the springs dried up. Complacent after the peril they had already lived through, most people refused to believe that the volcano would deal them the treacherous blow that seemed to be forecast by the rumblings and shakings and the fearful cattle and horses.

On August 24, A.D. 79, the mountain split and let out

a stream of fiery stones which set fire to everything they touched. Farms, villas, vineyards and towns were engulfed. The sea, disturbed by the earth movements, dashed ships to pieces in the harbour. Those who might have escaped being crushed to death by the falling buildings were almost certain to have met their deaths in the falling ashes or the rain of pumice (lapilli), or the gases which accompanied them. For 15 miles around the main crater the land was devastated.

The fall of Pompeii is one of the rare instances when historical evidence is exactly complementary to the archaeological evidence. The event is described fully by the younger Pliny, whose uncle perished in the eruption, and had sent out a detailed commentary during the days that preceded the final devastation. What history did not record about the tragedy, as well as many other pieces of information about life in the first century A.D. in the Roman Empire, is filled in by archaeological evidence.

The citizens had tried to flee—that much we can find in the pages of Pliny. But Pliny did not describe the beggar who was struck down as he fled and whose body outline was recovered during excavation. He had been wearing a pair of charity sandals—of good quality too—and a sack in which he carried the alms he had been given. This kind of detail of Roman life is difficult to find from historical sources. The Romans knew about the system of giving alms so there was little reason for them to write down a description.

One family were in the middle of a funeral feast—eating and drinking in the tomb of their ancestors—when disaster struck. The fine bronze doors of the chamber were blocked by the lava and the tomb of their ancestors became their own. Even the names of some Pompeians are known. The

A street scene from Pompeii. The Porta Marina (sea gate) almost exactly as it was in A.D. 79.

children found in the luxurious upper room of a town house were the offspring of Paquius Proculus.

Although August 24, A.D. 79, was no ordinary day, the remains chronicle accurately the daily lives of ordinary Romans. Although normally people would not have panicked or tried to bundle up their belongings, other aspects of life were represented more accurately than from most archaeological sites. Bread and wine was left on tables and counters—the fish and eggs that the priests of the temple of Isis were enjoying were almost intact.

The people who had lived in Pompeii and survived—probably about 18,000 out of the total estimated population of 20,000—would have set up home elsewhere. They would have gone to stay with friends or relatives and tried to forget the horror which had wrecked their lives. They would not have wanted to remember, and gradually the life that had once been enjoyed in the villas and hamlets in the 15-mile radius around the volcano would have been forgotten. It

A wooden chest from Herculaneum.

is true that some returned and tried to dig up their
belongings, but the 30 feet or so of lava rapidly turned to
a rock-like hardness and they had little success. The buried
cities were forgotten except for a vague memory of 'la citta'
among the local inhabitants who came eventually to till the
lands once the soil had reformed. Rumour of buried treasure
was carried on from generation to generation until the
barbarians overflowed the boundaries of the Roman
Empire and the old way of life ended completely.

Eventually men were attracted to the slopes of Vesuvius
in the Renaissance period. The ancient writers such as Pliny,
Martial and Dio Cassius had mentioned the destruction of
Vesuvius. The peaceful slopes seemed far removed from
such devastation, but the Italians dug hopefully. Then, in
1594, the Count Muzzio Tuttavilla decided to divert water
from the River Sarno to his villa. The route the channel
took happened to run through the Amphitheatre at
Pompeii, along the temple of Isis and through the Forum
(market square). The remains were not recognised as being
those of Pompeii, however, for another 30 years at least.

In the seventeenth and eighteenth centuries interest
became more fervent and digs were started to find out

whether the remains were indeed those of Pompeii. In the event, they found Herculaneum.

In 1710 a well was dug by a peasant which went into the city of Herculaneum. At this time Italy was in Austrian hands and the Count of Elbeuf had ordered a villa to be built nearby. He required objects to decorate his new home. When the peasant found marble objects in the well, the Count bought up the neighbouring land and set about excavating. Passages were bored through the remains with hopeless disregard for the damage that was being done. The theatre was discovered ready for the play, complete with scenery and staging. Everything removable was removed, though eventually work stopped and was resumed on the site of Pompeii, which had been discovered and recognised in the meantime.

The treasure hunts continued spasmodically until 1861, when Giuseppe Fiorelli undertook excavations which were a model of diligence and organisation for the time. Science was then making great strides and Fiorelli actually made a day-to-day account of the dig. Unfortunately he tended to recount which royal personages had been to visit them in preference to what objects were found and where. The excavations have continued, however, to the present day with increasing attention to modern methods.

The story of Pompeii and the neighbouring towns illustrates not only the way in which ancient sites can be lost and forgotten, but also how they were discovered during the pioneer days of the antiquarians. It is a splendid example of a site that is extremely well documented from archaeological and historical sources, so the historian and archaeologist can work hand in hand to mutual benefit. It is also one of the best instances where archaeology can produce much new material about a people who are well known from other sources.

12 ARCHAEOLOGY AND LEGENDS

GREEK LEGEND TELLS A STORY
of a king called Minos who demanded that every year
young men and maidens should be sent from the mainland
to his island home. They never returned to their homes.
The king had a son who was half a bull—a monster called
the Minotaur—who lived in a specially constructed labyrinth or maze and fed on the sacrificed maidens and youths.
Eventually, according to the legend, the Prince from Athens
was among the chosen victims. He borrowed a length of
twine from the king's daughter Ariadne and went into the
maze, unwinding it behind him. Inside the maze he killed
the Minotaur, rewound the twine and escaped.

How can this story have any truth? Excavations at
Knossos in Crete in this century by Sir Arthur Evans
suggested that it was based, albeit remotely, on fact. At
Knossos, Evans uncovered a palace which covered an area
of over 150 metres square. It consisted of room after room
leading off one another with open courtyards and magnifi-
cent stairways, royal apartments with fine wall paintings,
a throne room, artisans' workshops, storerooms and passages. The layout was indeed labyrinthine. Furthermore, in
the wall paintings were pictures of bulls. In the open main
courtyard was a pair of horns, strategically placed so that

View of the entrance porch to the Palace of Minos, Knossos, Crete, showing reconstructions of wall paintings.

the mountain in the distance rose between them. In the excavations fine carvings and models of bulls' heads were found—some lavishly ornate.

Could this have been the cult of a bull god? Sir Arthur Evans was certain that it was. Finally, some of the wall paintings showed extraordinary scenes of young men leaping in feats of acrobatics over the backs of charging bulls while young women stood by. The mystery seems to have been solved. Here was the original labyrinth of the legends. What had become distorted in folklore into a maze was, in fact, a complex palace with many rooms. The cult of the bull which demanded dangerous feats of prowess on the part of young people had become distorted in the telling into some mythical monster, half man, half bull.

The memory of the palace seems to have been lost soon after it was destroyed. Along with other palaces and settlements on Crete, the buildings were subjected to a destruction almost as complete as that at Pompeii. Whether this was due to a volcanic eruption or to an invasion from the mainland, or both, is still in dispute. But the fact remains

The stairway at the Palace of Minos, Knossos. The modern concrete pillars are painted red and replace the original wooden columns.

that the palaces were abandoned and the organised way of life ended. The people who tried to eke out a living in the same area in the subsequent centuries apparently forgot the life that had once been enjoyed in the palaces, except for the vague folk memory that was handed down in legend. By the nineteenth century only the legend remained.

The excavations revealed far more than the legend even hinted. The Minoans are known to have traded with the Egyptians. Ambassadors in Minoan dress have been found painted on the walls of the tomb of an Egyptian official, Rek-mi-re. The Minoans were great craftsmen—they made splendid jewellery and ornaments. They were able to carve difficult stones into intricate shapes. They had a distinctive style of wall-painting in vivid colours depicting dolphins and fish, princes and dancers. Much of our knowledge of Minoan religion comes from paintings of offerings being made at open-air shrines.

One of the most fascinating aspects about life under the Minoans was that there seems to have been no war. All the weapons found and the paintings or drawings of

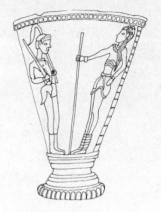

A handleless vase from Hagia Triada, Crete (a Minoan villa), showing a young prince giving orders to a subordinate officer.

weapons are of ceremonial types, that could only have been used in displays.

Minoan houses appear to have been constructed for defence against animals—the doors seem to have been built at least two feet above street level in the best preserved town of Gournia. A small picture of what is thought to be a house bears this out. The streets themselves were tortuous and narrow—only a donkey and pack could pass along them easily. The civilisation of the Minoans (so-called after the mythical King Minos) ranks among the greatest so far discovered, yet it was totally unexpected when it was found. Excavations still continue at Knossos and at other sites on Crete.

The legend of King Arthur and the Round Table has come into archaeological prominence recently. According to the old stories, King Arthur fought against the enemies of the Britons. He instituted an order of knights who sat in conference around a round table and who were pledged to fight for Good and Right. A thirteenth-century circular table in Winchester is still shown to visitors as belonging to King Arthur. The king was supposed to have lived in a castle—Camelot—and his knights wore armour, carried

A street with houses each side at the ruined Minoan town of Gournia, Crete.

banners, and fought with swords and spears. Many stories about the exploits of Sir Lancelot, Sir Kay, and Sir Bedevere and Arthur's queen Guinevere were made up in the Middle Ages and later.

This legend is possibly more credible at first than that of the Minotaur. But when research was carried out recently it was found that the origins of the legend lie in a period long before castles and knights came into existence.

It has been known for a long time that the Arthur of the stories was invented in the Middle Ages—probably in the twelfth century. It is almost certainly for this reason that so many places in Britain are associated with him. Medieval minstrels used to wander round the countryside singing songs and telling stories to the people. In order to please their listeners they made the events they were describing (and exaggerating) take place at some local landmark. No one wanted to hear about feats of courage and prowess that had been achieved many miles away by totally unknown men. Thus the Knights of the Round Table and King Arthur went down in folklore as living in places as far apart as Tintagel in Cornwall, Caerleon-upon-Usk in South Wales, and Arthur's Seat, Edinburgh.

South Cadbury hillfort, Somerset, showing the rampart remains round the hill top.

Before the Norman Conquest in A.D. 1066, relatively few people in Britain could read or write, and there is little mention of a King Arthur anywhere (there was certainly no King Arthur after 1066). The firmest evidence comes from a piece of writing that was set down in the tenth century, which refers to the year A.D. 518. This date lies between the withdrawal of the Roman troops from Britain by about A.D. 409 and the time when the Angles and Saxons who settled in the old Roman territories formed kingdoms (that eventually became England), in the seventh century. This is the general period during which the writer of the *Ruin* (p. 9) was alive and when very few people in Britain could read or write. It seems that Arthur was one of the local kings or leaders who fought against the Anglo-Saxons.

Many strongholds of the Britons of this period have been investigated by archaeologists and much is known of the Saxons and the Britons. It is known, for instance, that after

the Romans had left the Britons tried to carry on the
Roman way of life—for example, they organised the clean-
ing of town streets and the drainage systems. They seem to
have lived peaceably in many cases with the Anglo-Saxons
who settled in their regions. In fact there is very little to
suggest that all the incomers looted and pillaged wherever
they went, as the historical sources record. Many Anglo-
Saxon villages of the time did not even have fences around
them—suggesting that they were not afraid of attacks from
Britons.

Some Britons, however, were not so friendly either to their
British or their Anglo-Saxon neighbours. They returned to
the hillforts their ancestors had used before the Romans
had settled them in lowland towns. Places like Castle Dore
in Cornwall, and Chun Castle, were reoccupied in the Dark
Ages.

In 1966 excavations were carried out at a hillfort called
South Cadbury, in Somerset, which happened to be traditionally associated with Camelot and King Arthur.
Archaeologists led by Professor Leslie Alcock found that it
had been sacked by the Romans and then, in the Dark
Ages, a timber hall and strong defences had been built.
The hall showed up only from the remains of post-holes in
the ground. The defences could be reconstructed and were
found to be modelled on Roman types. This was another
instance of the inhabitants of the hillfort trying to keep up
the Roman ideal. Obviously, whoever lived in the hillfort
had enemies.

There was no real evidence which proved conclusively
that Cadbury was the original Camelot of the stories. Similarly, there was no evidence that a king called Arthur lived
there. But the story fitted the findings. Here at last, after
years of dispute and research, was a stronghold whose

chieftain was obviously a sworn fighter for the Britons (presumably against the Anglo-Saxons), who had a band of followers, and who lived in a timber hall. All the evidence of the finds and the stratigraphy led to the indisputable fact that the hillfort was used at about the time that the historical source states that Arthur was in operation. From all the evidence it has been possible to estimate that King Arthur was probably active between A.D. 475 and 515 and, if he did not live at Cadbury itself, he would have been very similar to the leader who used it.

Many other legends apart from that of the Minotaur and of King Arthur have been shown to have bases in fact by archaeology. The lost continent of Atlantis, for example, is thought to be Santorin. Some stories have been shown to have much less spectacular beginnings. A story of the lost Roman legion which is supposed to have marched north into Scotland never to return, is one such. The Ninth Legion disappeared from Roman records with no trace. Theories were brought forward to account for this— perhaps the legion had been lost dishonourably in a battle in the north and had been wiped out. Official records would not wish to record this shame. Archaeology, however, now suggests, from a tile from Nijmegen in Holland which is inscribed with the name of the Ninth Legion, that the end was not so dramatic. From this and other researches it appears that the legion became depleted after long campaigns and the remaining legionaries were absorbed into other parts of the army.

13 ARCHAEOLOGY AND THE RECENT PAST

WHAT DID YOU HAVE FOR dinner last Wednesday? If you can remember that, can you remember what you had for dinner on the second Wednesday of last month? Can you remember exactly what you said to everyone you met today? The answer, of course, is no. The greater part of everyone's own past is lost for ever, forgotten even by the person who experienced it, and the further back one goes in time the more is lost. That is why archaeology is not just useful for studying the remote past, but also has a part to play for studying very recent times. Even in our own century not everything is recorded, especially about everyday life. Even in the 1920s and 1930s detailed records were not always kept about what kind of commodities were sold most in particular areas, and archaeologists have been able to tell us from studying the rubbish in 50-year-old dumps more about the way of life of ordinary people than documents can.

Obviously, archaeologists do not spend a great deal of time investigating the remains of this century, but they are spending an increasing amount of time studying the remains of the seventeenth, eighteenth and nineteenth centuries. In Britain a great deal remains to be learned about the development of industry and the improvement of machines. Archaeologists excavate old potteries to find out what kind of kilns were used and to try to date the periods at which particular wares were being made. Big factories kept records that have survived, but many of the smaller centres of production are undocumented. At the time of writing, excavations are going on at pottery kilns at Buckley near Chester, and the results are being studied along with the written records to find out what kind of pottery was being produced there at what period.

Modern industrial development is constantly destroying old factories and warehouses, and old factory machinery is being replaced by new. Unless industrial archaeologists record such remains they will be lost for ever, and future generations may consider them far more important than any Roman villa or prehistoric fort.

In America, perhaps because there is documentary evidence only for a relatively short part of the past, archaeologists have been more conscious of the need to supplement the study of written sources with archaeology. One of the biggest post-medieval excavations in the world has been carried out over many years in Williamsburg in Virginia. Williamsburg was founded in 1632, and was the capital of Virginia from 1699 to 1779. In 1927 it was decided to restore it to its original eighteenth-century appearance, even down to the costumes worn, and over the years a great fortune has been spent on turning it into a showplace. The excavations in recent years have gone hand in hand with the restoration, and as a result more is known about everyday life in eighteenth-century America than in Britain.

Among the sites excavated was a shop occupied by a cabinet maker called Anthony Hay from 1756 to 1770. In the shop the excavators found the cabinet maker's tools—

awls, rasps, files, gauges, bits, plane blades and so on. They
also found bits of waterlogged furniture in various stages
of completion, including a walnut leg of a Chippendale
chair, the back leg of an armchair with its castor still
attached, and pieces of chests. They also found all sorts of
fittings from furniture—as some of them were old-fashioned
it seemed that Hay repaired old furniture as well as made
new, and it was also discovered that he bought brass fittings
in bulk and trimmed them to size.

Just how much information that archaeology can provide
which is not represented in documents can be seen by comparing the inventory of Hay's goods on his death with the
finds. Thirty-five types of objects in the inventory were
represented in the finds, and where the inventory only
listed 'two colored stone teapots' the archaeologists could
say that these were of Littler's blue stoneware which was
very rare at Williamsburg—only two examples have been
found in 30 years of digging there.

Another example of rewarding excavation on a site from
the recent past can be seen at Louisbourg in Nova Scotia,
Canada. Louisbourg was a fort built by the French in 1719,
which grew into an important town before being destroyed by the English in 1760. In 1960 it was decided to
restore the fort as a National Park, and excavation began
in 1961. The most sophisticated of modern excavation
techniques were employed. Archaeomagnetism was used for
checking the date of ovens (the dates were known from
history), and the 500,000 finds, from swords to chamber
pots, were analysed by computer and catalogued on punch-
cards—to deal with all the data a sophisticated retrieval
system was set up. Individual types of finds were examined
by metallurgists and others.

Autopsies were carried out on skeletons (most of whom

could be identified)—one had a crude metal filling in a tooth, carried out before 1745, while another had a 'false' tooth made from a pig's tooth inserted into the jaw.

By studying how compact the soil was in particular areas, the excavators worked out which had been thoroughfares across the open yard of the main fort. By testing the carbonate percentage in the soil they were able to detect a building—the lime mortar had decayed and the carbonate had been washed into the surrounding soil.

14 ARCHAEOLOGY AND THE UNKNOWN

LEGENDS AT LEAST PRESERVE some memory of ancient peoples, but many societies and several civilisations left no trace of their existence at all. Often their discovery has the most humble beginnings.

At a time when archaeologists had just started to make extensive use of scientific techniques, a site at **Star Carr** in Yorkshire was investigated by Professor Graham Clarke. The site might not at first have seemed very promising. In 1949, when the excavation was started, nothing was visible at ground level. Only the discovery of some flint implements and a few pieces of decayed antler and bone, during the cutting of a field drain, gave any clue to the existence of the remains of a Middle Stone Age (**Mesolithic**) campsite beneath the turf.

Fortunately for the archaeologists, the peat and organic mud had preserved many objects that would not normally survive from 9,000 years ago in Britain. Analysis of the organic finds—pollen grains, remains of plants, seeds, even shoots—built up a picture of the environment around the site. Apparently in the Middle Stone Age the village stood on the edge of a lake. Geologists and geographers added their knowledge to the findings. The bones found were analysed to find out what the villagers had eaten. (They split the bones to extract the marrow and ate mostly red deer.) Some of the bones were in such a fragile condition that a special apparatus was devised for impregnating them with a consolidant under vacuum conditions to enable them to be handled. The extent of the settlement was difficult to determine from the flimsy remains—it was calculated eventually by plotting the flints found on a map. Those areas of densest spread were calculated to be the main area of the village.

The picture that emerged was of a lake-side campsite in which about 25 people had lived (of whom about five were men capable of hunting). A platform had been built from logs around the edges of the lake on which the villagers had camped. It was possible to see from the way in which the logs were lying, which way the trees had been felled.

The villagers of Star Carr lived long before writing had been introduced to Britain. At about the same time, a people were flourishing at Catal Hüyük in Turkey, whose remains were equally forgotten, but whose standard of living was considerably higher.

One cold November day in 1958 as dusk was falling, a group of archaeologists arrived at two huge mounds in the Konya Plain of central Turkey. They were trying to make a systematic survey of all the sites in the region, and although the mounds had been seen from a distance in 1952, no opportunity had presented itself for them to examine them at close range. The two mounds were no ordinary hillocks. They covered about a third of a mile, and rose to a height of about 17·5 metres above the surrounding plain. When the archaeologists walked over the eastern mound they found the surface littered with patches of ash, broken bones, pieces of pottery and stone tools and weapons. In places the wind had stripped the surface of the mound and revealed traces of brick buildings burned red in some extensive fire. The mound was what the Turks called a *hüyük*—not the work of nature at all but the accumulation of the ruins of mud-brick buildings one on top of the other over a period of hundreds or thousands of years.

As he picked up pieces of pottery and tools the leader of the expedition, Mr James Melaart, got very excited. They all belonged to the **Neolithic** period—the New Stone Age —a period about which almost nothing was known in this part of Turkey. If that was not exciting enough, more remarkable was the fact that these Neolithic finds came not just from the bottom of the mound but from the very top as well. The remains he had discovered were those of a Stone Age city, built and rebuilt over a vast period of time.

From 1961 to 1963, when work was interrupted, Mr Melaart carried out a series of meticulous excavations on the site, which was known as **Catal Hüyük**. Gradually he began to reveal a small area of a city which shed new, exciting light on the origins of civilisation.

Mr Melaart knew better than to use the traditional methods of excavation generally employed in Turkey, which involved putting down trenches all over the mound until they reached the old natural ground surface. Instead he concentrated on excavating a small area of the mound totally, so that he could see the plans of the buildings in their successive stages. Had he not done so, he might have destroyed the unsuspected wall paintings and sculptures that adorned the shrines that he was to encounter, or he might have missed them altogether. As it was he was able to build up a clear picture of life in this one area of the mound, though his careful excavation meant that he never reached the earliest remains of occupation and never found out where the city workshops were or whether the houses were similar in different parts of the city.

Throughout the excavation the most modern techniques of excavation and analysis were employed. His team included a palaeobotanist (an expert on ancient plant remains), a physical anthropologist (an expert on skeletons), a textile expert, metallurgists, an expert on different types of wood, and conservation experts. In addition, Mr Melaart called upon experts on pigments, mineralogy, ornithology (bird remains), shellfish, and a variety of other things to report on his finds. Dates were obtained by radio-carbon techniques.

What sort of picture was pieced together of Catal Hüyük? It was a prosperous town which flourished before 6000 B.C. The square, flat-roofed houses were built out of bricks made from baked mud, a building material universal in the Near East where the sun is hot enough to bake the bricks and where there is little rain to turn them into mud again. None of the houses had doors; all were entered by means of a ladder from the roof, through a hole which also let the smoke out and light in. The only windows were just below the roof. This was because the houses were packed close together but were built on sloping ground so that each was at a different height from the others.

The people of Catal Hüyük were farmers, and by studying the remains of carbonised grains and animal bones the excavators were able to say what crops were grown, collected or brought in from the hills, and what animals were eaten. The finds in their shrines showed that they were concerned in their religion with the wild ox; it explains perhaps how people came to domesticate the ox and shows the first step towards the domestication of cattle. At first the citizens did not use pottery, but instead used baskets

and wooden dishes. Gradually, however, they began experi-
menting with clay for making pots, and here we can see
the beginnings of potting.

There were other firsts at Catal Hüyük, too—copper,
which is found in an almost pure state in Turkey, was
smelted and worked into beads, tubes and possibly small
tools. Lead, too, was worked. Most tools, however, were
still of stone. Many were very beautiful, and flint and
obsidian (a black volcanic glass) were imported for ceremonial knives and for making obsidian mirrors.

The most remarkable discoveries, however, were in the
shrines. In the area excavated there were almost as many
shrines as houses, and these were decorated with reliefs in
plaster (some modelled on the walls, the others cut into the
plaster when it was up), or painted with frescoes. Radio-
carbon dates showed that these shrines were in use between
6500 and 5700 B.C. The archaeologists found numerous
statues modelled in clay of goddesses and (less frequently)
gods, as well as some carved out of stone. One fresco showed
a town with houses in graded terraces (perhaps Catal Hüyük
itself), behind which a volcano was shown erupting.
Another showed a hunting scene. Paintings of insects and
flowers, of animals, and even of abstract patterns probably
copied from rugs were all encountered. One bizarre scene
showed vultures pecking at headless corpses. Most common
of all were representations of bulls' heads done in plaster,
or 'bucrania'—pillars adorned with bull horns. Of the
goddesses, the most popular perhaps was a 'Lady of the
Beasts', sometimes with leopards.

Many of the themes represented in the shrines can be seen
in much later times in the east Mediterranean. The
representations of bulls are very similar to those found in
the Bronze Age civilisation of Minoan Crete, some 4,000

years later, and indeed the goddesses with their animals are also found in Minoan art. There are hints, too, of the origins of many Greek myths in the representations—twin figures of goddesses recall similar figures in Bronze Age Greece and later Greek representations of the earth goddess Demeter and her daughter. Representations of butterflies are possibly the forerunners of the Greek butterflies that symbolised the spirit. Many of the paintings, however, looked backwards to the old Stone Age paintings of hunting scenes, and showed that the people of Neolithic Turkey were still concerned with hunting as much as with farming.

Taken as a whole, the excavations at Catal Hüyük show how hunting communities of the old Stone Age began to settle down and build cities, farm, and develop new crafts like potting and metalworking. Although older cities are known than Catal Hüyük (the oldest is Jericho in Palestine), and although evidence for domesticated animals and cultivated plants have been found at an earlier date further East, the finds from Catal show how these spread from the East to Europe, and how the seeds of later beliefs were already to be found 4,000 years before the flourishing of the great Bronze Age civilisations of the Mediterranean, such as that on Crete.

The most recent civilisation to come to light at the time of writing was found in September 1975 in Syria. Archaeologists digging at ancient **Ebla** (modern Tell Mardikh) found the audience chamber of the kings of Ebla, where they used to receive dignitaries and subjects. To one side of the chamber was a room which had been filled with rows of wooden shelves; 13,000–14,000 inscribed clay tablets filled the shelves. The language used on them was originally thought to be unknown but is similar to Sumerian,

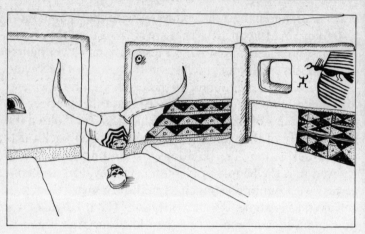

A reconstruction of the second vulture shrine in a house at Catal
Hüyük, Turkey. Painting adorns the walls, and a plastered bull's
skull faces a human skull.

so little difficulty is likely to be encountered in its de-
cipherment. Amongst the finds were the oldest known
dictionaries yet discovered—from Semitic to Sumerian and
vice versa. Textbooks on how to read and write, exercise
books and the teachers' marks were also found.

The full significance of this find will not be apparent until
the thousands of texts have been read and digested. What
is apparent at present is that Ebla was a power that was
hitherto unguessed. It seemed to have been a rival to the
other great Mediterranean state of Akkad which flourished
between 2350 and 2250 B.C.

15 ARCHAEOLOGY AND PERIODS OF HISTORICAL DARKNESS

MANY PERIODS IN THE PAST ARE mentioned only slightly in historical sources. Many legends originate in such times. Archaeology has been invaluable in shedding light in these cases. The Dark Ages in Britain, for instance, which were so called because historical sources were so sparse or confusing as to leave scholars in the dark, are no longer such an enigma. Archaeological studies have shown that many of the writings that came from this period, such as the poem the *Ruin* mentioned in Chapter 1, were either confused or incorrect.

The **Mote of Mark** is a small outcrop of rock rising about 100 feet above the coastline of southern Scotland. In February 1975 three archaeologists made their way to the top in the blustering wind and rain. They were seeking permission to excavate at the hillfort and were carrying out the preliminary reconnaissance. They were convinced that under the gorse and nettles lay the answers to several questions they had asked themselves about the site.

Around the top of the hill, now almost obscured by grass and gorse, ran a stone rampart. When had this been put up? Half-way down the slope lay piles of stones where the rampart had been demolished at some stage. When had this demolition occurred and why? The fort seemed to have

The Mote of Mark, Kirkcudbrightshire.

come to a violent end, since even before excavation the remains of a fire could be seen. Sticking up out of the grass in places were heaps of rampart stone which had been subjected to such an intense heat that the stone had melted and fused. Had this been caused by an accident or was it a deliberate act?

The site had already been excavated in 1913. The proposed excavation was to take place exactly 60 years later, and the results illustrate the advances made in archaeological science during that time.

The excavators wanted to redig some of the areas that the previous excavation had uncovered and to open up new areas. The excavator of 1913, Dr Alexander Curle, had produced a report that was highly detailed for the day, but he failed to mention, for instance, exactly where some of his trenches had been dug. His methods of digging, acceptable for the day, too, had been to leave a squad of workmen on the site all day digging, and to listen to their verbal

Stones of the rampart where they were thrown on to the side of the hillfort at the Mote of Mark.

Excavation in progress at the Mote of Mark, 1973.

reports in the evening. The careful records, scrupulous observation of stratigraphy and of findspots that are today's methods were unknown then. It is not surprising that Dr Curle mentioned in his report that he could see no stratigraphy at all; all the finds, from the earliest to the latest, appeared to come from the same layer. As a result, it was impossible, even by research on the finds in the Edinburgh Museum, to find out what had happened and when on the site.

When the excavation took place in 1973, many of these questions were cleared up. Many more were posed, however. It was found, for instance, that the rampart had been put up in the Dark Ages—not many centuries earlier in the Iron Age as had been suggested. Wooden posts burnt almost to charcoal, which Dr Curle had discovered and then covered over once more as being of no further use in 1913, were re-excavated and radio-carbon dating methods were applied. Unfortunately, only one could be taken and although the date arrived at was in the fifth or sixth centuries, it was not possible to be more precise than this about the date of the building of the rampart.

The bones of animals that Dr Curle had thrown back into the trenches were recovered. Since these had been touched by human hands in 1913 they were obviously too contaminated for radio-carbon dates to be found for them. They were analysed by a veterinary surgeon, however, and the diet of the people who lived in the hillfort was established. It was obvious that they lived on stews. Since no bones were found of the better cuts of meat, it was assumed that the animals were butchered elsewhere and steaks were brought to the site already filleted.

The site was already known to be a metalworking factory, since many clay moulds for beautiful and intricate jewellery and mounts for caskets were found in 1913. The Metallurgical Department at Liverpool University analysed the metal and shed much light on the methods of Dark Age smiths (p. 83), that were unknown previously.

The lack of stratigraphical layers noticed by Dr Curle with his methods of digging, was not noticed in the 1973 excavations. In the areas where no archaeologist had dug before, a cobbled yard was found—presumably these stones on other parts of the site were those described in the 1913 report as 'very stony soil'. When excavated carefully, however, they formed a pattern. It was even possible to establish where a hut had stood by the absence of cobbles in a circular area. Around the circular area were little heaps of stones which were all that had been left of the post-hole packing. On this site the weather had been so wet and the bedrock so acid that all other distinguishing marks of the layers had been removed. All the soil appeared to be the same colour and texture.

The results of the excavation are not yet fully analysed. The site was shown to be another instance of folklore preserving some element of truth, however. It was certainly occupied in the Dark Ages. The name Mote of Mark was given to the hillfort in the Middle Ages, probably by minstrels wandering around the area. King Mark was a common figure in the stories of King Arthur and the Round Table, which have been proved to belong to the same period. Why the fort was sacked is still in debate.

Aztecs, Incas, Mayas. The names conjure up for us a picture of lost cities in the jungle, of gold and of human sacrifice. These were the great civilisations of Central and South America, the civilisations discovered by the Spanish conquistadores in the sixteenth century, and which were to last but a short while after their discovery before their splendid cities were once more swallowed by the jungle and forgotten by all except a few of the descendants of the people who had once lived and died in them. Until a century ago virtually all that was known of these strange civilisations was what was recorded by the Spaniards, who were concerned more with converting them to Christianity and depriving them of their gold than setting down an accurate account of what they saw and what they were told about the ancient peoples.

Of all the ancient civilisations of America, one of the most remarkable was that of the Maya. Of all Mayan remains, the most splendid are those of their mountain capital of **Chichen-Itza**, the remains of which spread out over 12 square miles in the heart of the forest of the Yucatan peninsula of Mexico. Yet until the end of the last century nothing was known of Chichen-Itza, and it was not until an Englishman, Edward Thompson, began a long and painstaking series of excavations there around the turn of the century that the full splendour of the lost city became apparent.

The name Chichen-Itza means 'Well Mouth', and the most sacred place in the city was the great well of Yum Chac, the Rain God, who was said to dwell at the bottom of it. A Spanish writer described it to Charles V of Spain, saying that young girls were thrown into it to make requests of the rain god—some were dragged out again, but others drowned. They also threw in men as a sacrifice in time of drought, as well as precious stones, gold and prized belongings.

When Edward Thompson began investigating the well of Yum Chac it was clogged with centuries-old mud and decayed vegetation. It was a wide pool—160 ft. across at its widest point and from the lip of the pit to the very bottom was a drop of 130 ft. Thompson's workmen thought him quite mad to want to explore it. They dredged up bucket after bucket of evil-smelling muck and slime, empty of finds except for the bones of animals which had fallen by mistake into the pool. Day after day the workmen toiled, watched by frogs and lizards. Then, just when it seemed almost certain that the pool was going to prove quite empty, two lumps of resin came to the surface. This was as exciting a discovery as any pot or even of a piece of gold. For when Thompson lit a piece of the resin he found it gave off an aromatic smell. It was copal, which had been used for incense and burned before the girls were thrown into the pool. From that moment on discovery followed upon discovery.

Among the first of the finds was a rubber viper, which

looked so lifelike it terrified the workmen. Then came a bleached skull. Then another. Then another. Scores of human bones, mostly of young girls aged between 14 and 20, but occasionally of strong warriors, were dredged out of the pool. There were also treasures. Temple vases, incense burners, gold bells (deliberately flattened to throw into the pool), jade ornaments, beaten copper discs, some decorated with representations of the ancient gods of the Mayas, arrowheads, axes and hammers. When after months of dredging the scoop hit the bottom, divers went down into the murky depths of the oozing mud. So dark was it, the divers had to work by touch—their fingers contacted carved stone sculptures and the cold hardness of metal. When they emptied their pouches on the surface gold and green jade spilled out—gold tiaras representing feathered serpents, gold tops of official wands, jade rings and beads. The old stories about the well of Yum Chac had been proved true, and archaeology had not only verified written accounts, but had been able to elaborate upon them.

APPENDIX:
FINDING OUT MORE

Archaeology as a Career

Archaeology is a fascinating hobby, but does not make a very good career. To become an archaeologist it is usually necessary to go to university and study for a degree in the subject. Even with a degree, jobs are not easy to find, and the competition is very great. There are jobs in the civil service and in museums for archaeologists, as well as in universities, but the majority of jobs are for field archaeologists, usually attached to local authorities or excavation committees. Such jobs are seldom secure or well paid.

In contrast, archaeology is one of the very few professions in which amateurs can help—many important pieces of archaeological work have been done by people who have other jobs.

What You Can Do

Whether you want a career in archaeology or are just interested in it as a hobby, there is a lot you can do. This mostly involves recording sites, and the first two books on page 153 tell you how to set about doing useful practical work.

Joining a Dig

We have stressed in the book that excavation is a very technical business, and nobody should organise a dig without years of proper training. You must never dig for anything yourself, and should discourage others from doing so or report them to your local museum. Random digging is no better than vandalism.

That does not mean that you must not go on organised digs directed by experts. Many directors welcome young people, and often take on unskilled volunteers. Usually there is an age restriction—you have to be over 16 to work on the site because of insurance problems. Younger archaeologists, however, are often welcome to visit excavations and watch the work going on, and may even be given jobs like washing finds and sifting the spoil heap for fragments of pottery that have been missed.

Remember, if you are allowed to join a dig or visit it, that it is not a holiday camp but a scientific project. Always obey the site rules, and if you are visiting, do not disturb the diggers by talking to them or distracting them and do not go too near the edges of the excavated areas. Usually there will be notices up about areas you are not allowed to walk across. If in doubt, ask. Before visiting a dig write to the director and ask his permission to see it. He may suggest a particular time when someone will be available to show you around.

To find out about the digs that are in progress you can ask your local museum. A list of digs that welcome volunteers is also published by the Council for British Archaeology, and this comes out every month during the digging season (March to September). You can subscribe to it by writing to:

> The Council for British Archaeology,
> 7, Marylebone Road,
> London, N.W.1.

Local Societies

Many local archaeological societies flourish in Britain and these arrange lectures and sometimes visits to sites in the summer. A few run excavations. Most of them welcome young archaeologists, and you ought to join your local one in order to meet others with similar interests and to find out what is going on. Your museum will again be able to tell you who to write to. If you

have no local museum, a list of societies can be found in the
Archaeologist's Year Book (Dolphin Press).

Young Rescue

Every archaeologist under 16 should belong to Young Rescue,
a society designed specially for them. This publishes a regular
bulletin, *Young Rescue News*, which has articles from members
and from professional archaeologists, book reviews and news of
digs to visit. It arranges archaeological holidays, and has local
branches which hold meetings. For more details write to:

> Kate Pretty,
> c/o Dept. of Archaeology,
> Downing St.,
> Cambridge.

Finding Things

If you find something, perhaps in a field or garden, which you
think is of archaeological interest, you should make no attempt
to clean it except to brush off the earth gently (or wash it off
in the case of pottery or stone), and you must record exactly where
you found it and in what circumstances. Then take it along to
your local museum at the first opportunity. It may well turn out
to be very modern, but if it is, nobody will think you were silly
reporting your find, and you may have discovered something
which will radically change archaeological thinking! If you are
in the habit of finding things, or want to go looking for things,
you must observe all the rules about recording finds, about *not*
digging for them and about making sure you have permission
from the landowner first. All this is explained in our *Young
Archaeologist's Handbook* (Pan/Piccolo, 1976) and you ought to
read this first.

SOME SUGGESTED BOOKS

THERE IS SO MUCH TO KNOW about archaeology that no single book covers it all. Thousands of books and journals have been written on the subject, and you must decide which period or area most interests you and read books on that. Here we list a few general books and a few on some of the main subjects dealt with in the preceding pages.

General

Corcoran, J. X. W. P., *The Young Field Archaeologist's Guide* (Bell, 1976).

Laing, J. & L., *The Young Archaeologist's Handbook* (Pan/Piccolo, 1976).

(These are both practical books explaining what you can do.)

Ceram, C. W., *Gods, Graves & Scholars* (Penguin, 1974).

Ceram, C. W., *A Pictorial History of Archaeology* (Thames & Hudson, 1957).

DePaor, L., *Archaeology. An Illustrated Introduction* (Penguin, 1967).

Dyer, J., *Discovering Archaeology* (Shire, 1969).

Kenyon, K., *Beginning in Archaeology* (Phoenix, 1953).

Magnusson, M., *Discovering Archaeology* (Bodley Head, 1972).

Special Topics

Feachem, R., *From Windmill Hill to Hadrian's Wall* (W. & A. K. Johnson, 1961).

Place, R., *Prehistoric Britain* (Longmans, 1970).
Roe, D., *Prehistory* (Paladin, 1971).
Wood, E. S., *Collins Field Guide to Archaeology* (Collins, 1963).
   (All the above lay emphasis on Britain.)

Brion, M., *Pompeii and Herculaneum* (Elek, 1960).
Glob, P., *The Bog People* (Paladin, 1971).
Hay, J., *Ancient China* (Bodley Head, 1973).
Higgins, R., *Archaeology of Minoan Crete* (Bodley Head, 1973).

INDEX